Driving Bus Number 7

A true story of love, respect and admiration

By Renee Joseph

Jill,
Finally after five years my book is complete. Hope you enjoy!
Warmest regards,
Renee
2019

Self-published — AMAZON
November 2018

Dedication
To my Dad and Mom whose love and admiration for humankind was an inspiration for many.

Table of Contents

Prologue

Butterflies – The First Day of School

The Early Years

Driving School Bus - the Journey Begins

Hardship

A New Beginning

A Switch in Career and Focus

Leaving the Farm for City Life

Settling into "Semi-retirement" Life

Illness Strikes my Dad

Dad's Battle to Beat Cancer is On

Home at Last

Dad in Good Health when Tragedy Strikes

Cancer Returns but First We Must Honor Mom

Time to Address Cancer AGAIN

Heart Issue

Cancer Tightens Its Grip

Time to Hang Up Bus Number 7 Keys

Time to Celebrate Richard

Epilogue

Driving Bus Number 7

Faces in the rear view mirror

Prologue

What would motivate a man to drive a school bus for fifty-three years? "Bus Number 7," his lucky number, was the bus he always drove. In fact he chose to drive virtually the same route for all of those fifty-three years. This man happens to be my father, and this book recounts his fifty-three year journey. It is a journey that takes place in rural Wisconsin, very near a town called Westby, with a man who began with a total dislike for driving a school bus and ended with "his Bus Number 7 kids" being his motivation for getting up in the morning. As it turns out, "his Bus Number 7 kids" became one of his main reasons for living.

My father was a dedicated, determined man who was a role model for his four children and an inspiration for three generations of bus families as well as an entire community.

This book is a collection of stories and memories gathered during my father's long battle with cancer. Many of the stories Dad shared firsthand with me during the many hours we spent together as he underwent treatment for non-Hodgkin's lymphoma. The rest came from firsthand accounts from current and past school riders and family members of Bus Number 7. This truly is a story of love, respect, and admiration.

Butterflies – The First Day of School

The hot muggy days of late August suddenly give way to the crisp, clean mornings of September. The corn fields, heavy with the soon-to-be-harvested crops, sway gently in the wind. The once lush green hayfields are now "clean shaven", mellow and ready for a long winter's nap.

Dad's bus route begins approximately two miles outside of Westby, traveling across an area called Lovaas Ridge. On this particular morning, Lovaas Ridge sparkles with the morning dew while the nearby valleys are shrouded in fog and mist. The rural Wisconsin county road running north and south is barren except for the long shadows cast by the autumn sun against the school bus and the sounds of Bus Number 7. Towering above the noise of the school bus engine is the unmistakable sound of country music. It is none other than Johnny Cash, his deep raspy bass voice blaring "I'll Walk the Line" from the less-than-Bose-quality radio speakers of the bus.

Another voice equally deep in timbre but slightly off key and out of rhythm accompanies Johnny's every word. The voice is that of the bus driver; Richard Ekern, my Dad. The year is 1953. It is Dad's first day at the wheel of bus number 7 and today is the first day of school.

For a child growing up in rural America, their first exposure to school is typically riding a school bus. For many children, it is also the first time they are away from their parents and "technically" on their own. Imagine the feeling. An enormous bright yellow bus comes lumbering into your driveway, the doors swing open, and a "stranger" from behind the wheel suddenly welcomes you on board. That's it. Find a seat, wave to Mom and Dad, and away you go. You barely have time to catch your breath when the bus has turned around and you are leaving your home.

You are now officially off to school surrounded by kids of all ages, most of who you do not know, in a bus driven by someone you also do not know. Talk about overwhelming and more than a little intimidating, even for the bravest youngsters.

And so, the cycle begins. From this day forward for pre-school age 4 until high school graduation age 17 or 18, the bus and the driver are the beginning and end to almost every day of school.

Little do the kids know that for first-time bus drivers, such as my Dad, they are probably equally if not actually more nervous and intimidated than the kids riding the bus are. This was very much the situation in Dad's case. You see, he did not really want to drive bus. Driving school bus was not something that he had ever, not even once, considered doing with his time. His decision to become a school bus driver was driven solely out of necessity and a deep sense of obligation to our family. He was driving bus as a means to an end. Driving school bus meant that he was able to provide health insurance for our family.

The Early Years

My Mom, Ilene Egstad, and Dad, Richard Ekern were high school sweethearts. They were married just shy of two years after graduating from Westby High School. Dad was the confident, slightly cocky athlete from rural Chaseburg and Mom, well, she was the petite, slender, well-behaved young woman being raised by her grandparents.

They first met in high school algebra class where Mom sat directly in front of Dad. In those days, classrooms were typically arranged alphabetically by last name. This meant that Mom, last name Egstad, was sitting directly in front of Dad, last name Ekern. Mom had politely turned around and asked Dad to open a window as the air in the classroom was quite stale.

Dad had curtly replied that if she wanted the window opened then she should open it herself. Mom was appalled by this abrupt reply and proceeded to tell him how incredibly rude he was. While this was certainly not exactly the ideal way to start a relationship, it ended up resulting in fifty plus years of marriage.

I guess the fact that Mom and Dad sat in such close proximity for every class for all four years of high school provided them ample opportunity to heal this wound and develop a relationship. They grew to appreciate their differences although their strong personalities were always quick to surface.

As it turned out, math was Mom's weakest subject. She had great difficulty with geometry and once again found herself turning to the person sitting immediately behind her (Dad) for help. Although reluctant at first, he agreed to help her and was proud of the fact that her grades improved immensely. Mom also admitted that without Dad's help, she would have certainly failed the class. He took great pride in knowing that this was the case and never missed an opportunity, even many, many years later, to remind her of that fact. Good thing they both had a good sense of humor.

Their first official date came in the summer of 1948. Dad sent Mom a penny postcard asking her to go with him to a July 4th festival that was being held in Coon Valley, a town that happened to be about halfway between Westby and Chaseburg which was Dad's hometown. Should she accept, they would be double dating with Dad's good friend and his girlfriend, both of which were also friends of Mom's. When the postcard arrived, her grandfather, a conservative Norwegian, intercepted it and promptly proceeded to tell her that she would not be able to go.

Mom's mother, Anna, died shortly after giving birth to Mom. According to Anna's obituary, "she died of a weakened state as the result of rheumatic fever several days after giving birth." Anna was the oldest child of Nordahl and Rena Egstad. At the time of her death, Anna's husband and everyone involved decided it would be best for the child, Ilene Ann, to live with Nordahl and Rena with no further contact with her maternal father or his family. Nordahl and Rena lived approximately three miles outside of Westby on a small dairy farm which was the homestead for the Egstad family after emigrating from Norway to the United States in the 1800's.

Nordahl and Rena had three other children Martin, Norman and Ruth. Mom was being raised by her grandparents with aunts and uncles who she considered to be her brothers and sisters. Mom's childhood was filled with a grandfather who adored her and a grandmother who certainly loved her but who was not exactly enamored with raising yet another child. She had already been mother to and had raised four children who were now in their late teens and early adult years when Mom arrived. As you can imagine, they loved having a new addition to the family.

Rena, however, had eagerly awaited the birth of their first grandchild and was looking forward to assuming the role of grandmother. With Anna's sudden death, however, that was not to be the case. Now quite late in life she found herself once again caring for and raising an infant.

Although Mom's siblings were actually her uncles and aunt, they would grow up to love and treat each other as brothers and sisters. During the early years they were a great source of help and companionship. Martin loved to bundle Mom up and pull her on his snow sled. Norman would take her horseback riding and Ruth would play house with Mom for hours on end. Within a few short years however they had each graduated from high school and had left the farm to begin their own adult lives. This left Nordahl and Rena as sole caregivers for Mom.

With no siblings left living at home, Mom spent as much time as she could with Nordahl. He was a patient man who enjoyed teaching Mom about farm life and loved her nonstop chatter. He was more relaxed and available to her than he had been with his own children given that they were now financially independent and well established. Rena on the other hand was a good caregiver but was no longer interested in the teaching aspect of motherhood. Showing Mom how to make cookies, bake bread, or preparing a meal was really out of the question. Any such efforts were sure to cause a mess and undoubtedly slow down her routine. Instead of teaching Mom to sew or knit, she preferred to just do it herself. Mom learned at an early age that it was much more fun to be around Nordahl and whenever possible she would give Rena her space.

Her school days were spent at Clockmaker School. Clockmaker was a two room country school about a half mile from their home. There were two teachers for the entire school; one taught grades one through four and the other fifth through eight. While her siblings had to walk to and from school, Nordahl saw to it that Mom either rode with neighbors or he would take her to and from school himself. Mom recalls that one spring morning she and several other kids decided to skip school. Rather than going into their classroom they had spent the entire day at a nearby stone quarry. Much to her surprise the teacher had contacted Nordahl and Rena about her absence. When she returned home to the farm that day both Nordahl and Rena were waiting for her. As her punishment she had to go back to school and apologize to her teacher. She said it was the toughest and most valuable lesson of her young life.

Mom knew in the back of her mind that she had Nordahl wrapped around her little finger but she also knew how protective he was when it came to boys. It was no surprise to her when he had abruptly told her she was not allowed to go out with Richard even before she had had a chance to read his postcard. Once she had read the invitation, she just quietly put it aside. No need to get everyone all worked up, she thought to herself; at least not until it was absolutely necessary.

The day of the festival arrived and since Dad had not heard any different he and his friend proceeded to drive his friend's car to the farm and pickup Mom. Dad eagerly walked toward the house only to find Nordahl greeting him at the door. Before Dad could even formally introduce himself, Nordahl announced that Mom would not be going anywhere that evening.

Mom, watching this scene unfold from her second story bedroom window quickly opened the window and stated that she would be right down. Nordahl closed the door and went inside. Several minutes passed before Mom came waltzing through the door with her coat draped carelessly over her shoulder. Nordahl who was standing directly behind her gave Dad a slight wave and reminded them both of her curfew. Mom gave Nordahl a quick wink, a big hug and off they went.

Dad's childhood was a mix of tough love and hard work. Number two son out of six children, Dad grew up on a small dairy farm in Dodson Hollow which is in rural Chaseburg. His mother Martha was the dominant force in his family. A stoic religious Lutheran, she believed strongly in the benefits of hard work. She routinely woke at 5 am or before and made sure that the rest of the family was up and ready for the day before sunrise. No funny business to be had in this household.

Dad's father Lawrence however, was a gentle quiet man who did what he had to in order to keep peace in the family and on the farm. He was known to occasionally visit the taverns in nearby Chaseburg enjoying a beer or two while playing the fiddle. Martha considered both these pastimes to be "sins". It was a good thing Lawrence had good friends who were able to keep these little adventures a secret.

At an early age my father's sister Eunice and brother Merlin contracted tuberculosis. They were sent to a sanitarium in Madison until they were well enough to return home. Times were tough requiring everyone to pitch in and do whatever was necessary to make ends meet. Dad and his siblings were expected to help with all the farm duties, plant and harvest crops and even take care of providing food for the family by routinely catching fish in the nearby creek.

In order to further supplement the families' income, Dad and his older brother would do farm work and field work for neighbors. The expectation was that the money received for providing these services would be put into the "family kitty" however, this was not always the case.

Dad and his siblings, Gordon, Merlin, Eunice, JoAnn and Burton went to Linrud country school, a two room school house which taught grades one through eight. They walked or rode bike to and from on most days which meant that with a little creativity you could actually skip school without getting caught. Dad recalled how he and his older brother Gordon, used some of the money they had earned to buy a train ticket and go to La Crosse and play pool all day. They "hitchhiked" to Chaseburg, caught the outbound train to La Crosse and returned just in time to get back to the farm in time for evening chores. In order to not have their other siblings "squeal" on them, they had to pay them off as well. Thank goodness Martha never really understood how much they earned working for the neighbors. As you can see Dad's entrepreneurial style developed at a very early age.

Ninth grade for all the area schools meant it was time to go to Westby High, a small school with approximately 50 kids in their graduating class. It was in the ninth grade when Dad and Mom's lives would intersect. Westby high school was the center of their activities for the next four years. As you can imagine, this meant that everyone knew everyone and most everything that was going on. Mom and Dad ran in the same circles even dating each other's best friends on and off throughout the four years. For Mom there was cheerleading, band, and yearbook. For Dad sports, sports and more sports. Together they participated in the drama club which was their first real chance to spend any nonacademic time together.

Immediately following graduation Dad worked at the feed mill in Chaseburg grinding feed and loading trucks most of the day. Mom worked in the office at The Trane Company. They were constantly in touch and on February of 1952 after a short engagement they were married.

Immediately following their marriage they moved to Rockford, Illinois where Dad planned to make "big" money working at an ammunition production plant. The ammunition was being used to help fight the Korean War. They lived in a small apartment where Mom did her best to make their house a home. Having not had any childhood experience in the kitchen this proved to be interesting. Much later in life Dad recounted Mom's first home cooked meal; a baked chicken with all the trimmings. They both laughed hysterically as they recalled the dining room table (actually a card table) adorned with candles, linens and their brand new sterling silverware. An entire chicken complete with stuffing was positioned in the center of the table. Potatoes, gravy and Dad's favorite, corn, rounded out the meal. Picture perfect, perhaps, but eating it was going to be another story. Despite Dad's best efforts, utilizing their brand new carving knife which they received as a wedding gift, he was unable to carve let alone dent the chicken. Nothing could permeate the bird. Mom confessed that she had bought a stewing chicken thinking that if she cooked it long enough it would turn out tender. Boy was she wrong. Giving up on the chicken, they instead dined on the chewy potatoes, lumpy gravy and according to Dad delicious corn. He had ranted and raved about the corn helping to boost Mom's spirits. So would end their first major meal. Little did Dad know that this meal was actually a premonition of many of the meals they would have throughout their lifetime.

It was shortly after this that Mom began to not feel well. A quick trip to the Doctor had confirmed what at least Mom had expected. They were going to have a baby. Mom was pregnant and suffering from morning sickness. This was a difficult time for them. They were used to a lot of family and friends and now found themselves pretty much alone. Dad was working long hours so Mom did her best to ready their tiny apartment for their soon to be baby and befriended an elderly neighbor lady. Reid was born and their eager anticipation suddenly gave way to the reality of caring for a rather fussy baby. Dad soon realized that factory work was not for him. Mom too was not happy in Rockford and longed to return to family and friends. So they decided to return to the Westby area.

They packed up their few worldly processions, most of which they had received as wedding gifts, and returned to the farm where Nordahl and Rena had agreed to let them temporarily live. Despite the fact that they had a baby to care for, no job, and very little savings in the bank neither one of them, especially Dad was not overly concerned. He was a confident man who was sure that he would be able to find some kind of work that would suit him and was sure that Mom and Reid would do better back in Wisconsin with family and friends.

Luckily for them, Nordahl and Rena had been considering selling the farm but had not come to terms with giving up the homestead. They were both advanced in their years and knew that the time had come where dairy farming was no longer feasible. Nordahl was getting too old to keep up with milking dairy cattle and all the chores that went along with that type of farming. Shortly after Mom and Dad returned to the farm, Nordahl had casually mentioned selling the farm to Dad and Mom. Dad was eager to jump at the chance but Mom wasn't quite so convinced. She by nature was more conservative than Dad and thought that buying the farm would not only be financially very difficult for them but would also be too much work. After several rounds of discussion Dad was convinced that this was the right thing to do. Mom finally relented. Thanks to Nordahl's influence and good standing with the local banker they were able to get the necessary bank loan and as a result were now the proud owners of the Egstad homestead. Nordahl and Rena moved to a small house in Westby.

For Mom and Dad the early years of dairy farming certainly supported the old saying "if something can go wrong it will go wrong" theory. Shortly after buying the farm several cattle got sick and a major hail storm damaged some of the crops. Then the manure spreader quit working. This was the ultimate insult as it would be to most farmers. Not only was working the farm and growing the crops proving to be extremely hard work; now he couldn't even get the cow "poop" spread onto the fields.

Nordahl knew the toll that farming could take on a couple and kept close tabs on how things were going. He seemed to know just the right time to come to the rescue. He was a kind and generous man and had grown especially fond of Dad. In the case of the manure spreader, he had quickly gone to the local farm implement dealer and purchased a brand new spreader. He even had it delivered directly to the farm to add an element of surprise for Dad. He teased Dad saying that Dad could pay him back from "all" the money he had saved while working at that "fancy" factory in Rockford. This remained a joke between them for years. It was obvious that Grandma Nordahl was especially glad to have them return to the area and was thrilled to have the homestead remain in the family.

The homestead that Dad and Mom farmed was quite small. There were about 60 acres about half of which was woodland. They were dairy farmers which meant they had about 40 cows that had to be milked twice a day, preferably being milked at the same time every day. As I mentioned earlier, this was a demanding way to make a living. Milking cows twice a day, seven days a week, three hundred and sixty-five days a year meant here was no time for vacations or even a day off. In addition, the cows had to be fed, bedded and young stock tended to. There were crops to be planted, fertilized, cultivated and harvested. Machinery as well as barn, out buildings and the house were in constant need of repair or maintenance. Dairy farming is truly one of the original 24/7 type of careers.

For those of you that are not familiar with dairy farming, selling cow's milk to a creamery is a farmer's primary source of income. Crops are grown and harvested for the primary purpose of feeding the cattle. Rarely is there any corn or hay left over to sell on the open market. Therefore the "milk" checks are what farmers live on.

In addition to the demands of farming and raising crops, most farmers also had to be a "jack of all trades" as most could not afford to hire professionals to take care of electrical, plumbing and general carpentry needs. This was especially true in Mom and Dad's case as money was extremely tight.

As a result my father became a self-taught electrician, plumber and carpenter. He also, out of necessity, became a self-proclaimed veterinarian tending to sick cows and calves. In the business of farming, where your cattle generate your income, you cannot afford to not treat immediate medical needs of the animals. Whether this meant helping a cow deliver a breach calf in the middle of the night or performing emergency surgery to prevent an animal from dying, my father like most other farmers in the area, became very resourceful.

Driving School Bus - the Journey Begins

Two years after buying the farm, I was born. The year was 1954 and times were tough. Milk prices are a perfect example of supply and demand and during this particular period in time supply was very high compared to demand. As a result, the price paid to farmers for their milk was extremely low. "Milk" checks, our primary source of income barely covered the costs of the basics such as food and clothing. If there was ever any money left over it was almost always used to repair or replace a broken piece of farm equipment or pay down a medical bill. Being able to afford health insurance was out of the question.

It was during this time that Dad with a wife and two children decided he had to do something in order to provide his family health insurance. While at the local Westby feed mill one morning, he heard a couple of guys say that the Westby school district was in desperate need of drivers for the upcoming school year. They said that in addition to a small salary drivers were given the same medical insurance and benefits as teachers. Dad was eager to see if this was in fact true. Even before talking with Mom about the idea he drove to the high school and talked with the school administrator about the job. The administrator confirmed what he had been told by the two guys at the mill. In addition to a small salary, health insurance was included as a benefit; and they were in fact desperate for drivers. Dad returned home and explained the situation to Mom. He was sure that by getting up an hour or so earlier each day and adjusting his daytime schedule that he would be able to handle driving school bus. They really had no choice, he explained to Mom. Going without health insurance was really too risky. He would drive school bus out of necessity. The salary would be a nice supplement to their living expenses and most importantly he would be able to provide health insurance for our family.

Although Mom was not very excited about him taking on another job, as dairy farming was already a demanding 24/7 job in itself, she knew that Dad had already made up his mind. There was really nothing more to be said. It was what he had to do for his family. He applied for the job and learned that very same day that he was hired.

Now, in addition to the trades he accumulated from farming he added school bus driving to his repertoire. My father rarely complained. For the most part he merely took things in stride and focused on what he had to do to care for Mom and our family. This was until he learned that there was no real training for the position of bus driver. It was what would be called the ultimate on-the-job training. If you had a valid driver's license and were not a convicted felon you were hired.

With this news now sinking in, you can understand Dad's trepidation with the first day of school. He had never driven bus before, had no experience with school age children and was uncertain of his route; talk about intimidating. He was however now officially an employee of the Westby School District and was the driver of "Bus Number 7". He was responsible for safely picking up and delivering just fewer than 50 kids, ages 4 through 18, to and from school each and every day of the school year. He knew that he needed to do whatever it took to hide his anxiety.

In preparation for the big day, he decided to test drive his bus route using his own car. He did this several times the week before school started pretending as best he could he was doing an actual run. He created a "cheat sheet" complete with names, addresses, and his personal comments about handling the bus during the descent from the ridge top to the valley. His route consisted of mostly gravel roads which were extremely narrow and curvy. Most of the driveways were not exactly designed to turn a sixty passenger bus around. He knew that performing this feat was going to take his total concentration and driving skills. He made detailed notes about how he was planning to turn around in cramped quarters and soon realized that his biggest concern was about how much time it was going to take him to complete his route. His goal was to avoid any serious miscues on the first day of school, especially being tardy with a bus load of kids on the first day of school. He really did not want to look like a rookie.

The day before the big day arrived he set his alarm for 4:30 am. He wanted to make sure that he had plenty of time to milk the cows and do morning chores before showering, having breakfast and taking his place behind the steering wheel of Bus Number 7. He had meticulously planned his entire morning. What he had not counted on however was the nerves that set in the night before. Just as they turned out the lights for the night and settled into bed, his mind began to race. He tossed and turned for most of the night. He watched the clock as time crept along. He was relieved when the clock finally said 3:48 am. He grabbed the clock from the nightstand and turned off the alarm so as to not wake Mom. He went about getting the farm chores taken care of focusing on the task at hand so as to not get too distracted about what was to come. Finally with the farm chores taken care of, he showered, ate breakfast and had time to spare as he drove to Westby in his old Ford pick-up. He replayed the route in his mind and tried his best to recite from memory the names and ages of the kids at each stop. He soon realized that his memory was not going to be his friend that day. He was much too nervous for this to happen. Instead he decided that his cheat sheet would in fact be his best friend and that he would need to rely on it heavily if he had any chance of accomplishing his goal; no serious miscues on the first day.

He was as apprehensive as one of his kindergarten kids, behind the steering wheel of Bus Number 7. He buckled his seat belt, tuned the radio to his favorite country station and cranked up the volume to help calm his nerves. Away he went. Methodically he made each stop taking great care to double check his cheat sheet before greeting each child by name, introducing himself and asking how their summer vacations had been. Before he knew it, he had picked up and successfully delivered 40+ bustling kids to school. No major missteps. An occasional stall while trying to maneuver the bus in the tight quarters of some of the driveways; but other than that he had accomplished his goal with several minutes to spare. He was proud of his accomplishment and was especially thankful that he had not forgotten anyone.

Mom was eager to know how his morning had gone and was waiting at the door for him when he returned from his route. Over an early lunch Dad shared highlights of the morning route explaining how tough it had been to balance concentrating on driving while dealing with the constant noise and commotion 40+ kids can cause. Then as was normally the case immediately following lunch he took his traditional thirty minute nap. He woke abruptly after exactly thirty minutes realizing that there was a lot of work that still needed his attention. Ripe crops were in dire need of his attention. Once crops are ready to be harvested there is really not time to wait. The smallest wind storm or heaven forbid a hail storm could wipe out an entire seasons worth of crops.

He immediately went to tend to the fields and just as he started to make progress he realized that it was time to head back to school for the return trip. It was already after 2:00 pm and he had not yet left the farm. He quickly changed out of his "barn" clothes, jumped in his truck and drove the three miles to town. He arrived just in time to drive his bus from the bus garage up to the school. There he took his place in the bus lineup and waited patiently for the dismissal bell to ring and the children to appear.

Many of the other veteran drivers had congregated outside their buses. They were laughing and chit-chatting about the weather and who knows what else. Dad however remained huddled inside his bus. It had just dawned on him that he not given any thought to the return trip. He had been so caught up in the morning route that he had not considered the changes that would need to be made for the return route. He now faced the task of reversing the route and delivering the kids safely to their homes. Ok, he thought to himself this can't be that difficult. Last kid on in the morning was to be the first kid off in the evening. This sounded simple enough however it proved to be the most challenging part of the day. Reversing the route and dropping the kids off was not the problem; but rather the actual driving of the bus. You see the return route meant that rather than driving the bus down from the ridge top to the valley he now had to navigate the bus up from the valley to the ridge top. Going up the steep narrow gravel road from the valley to the ridge top meant that he had to be constantly shifting the bus and adjusting his speed to accommodate the twists and turns. Twice he had killed the engine. He worked hard to keep his composure as he restarted the engine. Just as he was starting out again, the bus began to jerk and buck. He was struggling to achieve the delicate balance between releasing the clutch and managing the brake. He was an experienced driver conquering the clutches of the various tractors he had driven over the years; but the bus system seemed to have a temperament all its own. He made light of the entire event so as to not alarm the kids.

Finally, with the last kid safely delivered to his home he let out a huge sigh of relief. As he drove the final stretch of highway that remained between his route and the bus garage he suddenly realized how exhausted he was. The stress of driving coupled with the noise level of the kids had taken its toll. He parked his bus, jumped in his Ford pick-up, kicked up the volume on his radio an extra notch and slowly drove home. He was enjoying this time knowing that as soon as he returned to the farm it would be time to once again milk the cows and do the evening chores. It was then that Dad realized what a juggling act it was going to be to both drive bus and farm. Finally just before 10 pm he crawled into bed. Just before falling to sleep his reset his alarm for 4:30 am and vowed that tomorrow would be a better day.

So began a routine that would continue for most of Dad's life. That day was the start of what would become a lifetime (fifty three years) of driving Bus Number 7. He was driving purely out of necessity. He dreaded the disruption to the already too busy farm day and was deeply annoyed by the boisterous spunky kids. The kids were just kids. They were merely names and addresses; faces in his rear view mirror. He was paid to do a job pure and simple. Pick them up in the morning and deliver them to school safely and on time followed by picking them up from school on time at the end of the day and delivering them safely home.

Hardship

Two years into driving school bus, Mom and Dad learned they were going to have another child. Thankful for the health insurance that they continued to obtain as a result of Dad's bus driving job, they eagerly welcomed Randy into our family. Now, with three children in the family, each of us two years apart, every dollar of income Dad earned from farming and bus driving was used to pay for the necessities of life. He offered to drive additional bus routes for extracurricular events such as baseball games or musical events with the hopes of starting a savings account. Shortly after establishing an account with the local bank and depositing their first amount, hardship struck our family.

Our farm was located at the top of a ridge with a view spanning for several miles. Most of the time this meant awe inspiring sunrises from the east and reflective sunsets from the west. That was the good news about living in such a panoramic location. The not so good news was that if there was any kind of thunderstorm we were the first to see it coming and feel its wrath. In fact our farm had such an expansive view the local weather station positioned a weather crew on the highest point of the farm. These "storm chasers", as we called them would help determine a storm's intensity and speed. They would use this information to determine when to issue weather watches and warnings in our part of Vernon County.

Today the skies were deceiving. What had started out as a bright and beautiful day would turn out to be a dark and bleak afternoon. Our two-story farmhouse was over a hundred years old and was partially built of log. The basement was only accessible from outside the house through a set of double doors which triangulated from the ground. Once inside the cellar, the space was cool, dark and damp. The earthen floor was uneven and littered with rocks and stones. The stone walls were cracked and needed to be repaired. In one corner was a root cellar with canned fruits and vegetables jars filling almost all of the shelves. The rest of the basement was mostly empty except for an overused-overstuffed grey arm chair which had been previously been in my grandparent's living room, a transistor radio, a flashlight and some old comic books. The chair was strategically placed in the southwest corner; the location my Mom had determined to be absolutely the safest spot for us to wait out any storms.

You see my mother was deadly afraid of storms. Throughout our childhood it was quite common for her to wake us at the first sound of thunder. Even in the middle of the night, in the midst of a dead sleep she would rouse us up for the purpose of shuffling us outside into what she called the storm cellar. She had been the one to "furnish" the storm cellar with what she called the necessities. The old chair, the radio, flashlight and comic books, those had all been her idea.

My dad on the other hand did not share the same level of concern with regard to storms. He did however, as he did most of their married life, know when it was best to just go along with what Mom wanted. He was for the most part pretty laid back and did what he could to minimize tension and stress in their relationship. He had accommodated her need to construct a storm cellar moving the old-overstuffed grey arm chair into the basement with so much as a hint of a complaint. He had even made sure that there were always fresh batteries on hand in a box in the basement for the radio and flashlight should the need arise.

As children we had also learned it was usually easier to just go along for the ride than object to my mother's concerns. This was especially true when it came to storms and bad weather. We had become so accustomed to late night/early morning frantic wake-up calls that we could rise to attention without becoming fully awake. We could make the trip down to the main floor, outside the house and down the cellar steps without missing a beat. Once inside, the three of us would merely curl up in the grey chair and resume our sleep. Only on rare occasions did we become alarmed and join Mom in her harried frenzy.

So late in the afternoon of what had been a beautiful Sunday as we heard my mother's frantic call, we knew something was seriously wrong. She was telling us to come to the house immediately. We could tell by the urgency in her voice that we had better not dawdle, a word my mother loved to use. My brothers and I were in the haymow of the barn playing hide and seek and hadn't noticed the change in the weather. The once baby-blue powder puffed sky had changed into a threatening blue-grey-black color with a dark haze on the entire landscape. The sky looked as though it had been in a terribly fight; all bruised and battered. The thunderheads were building and gaining strength at an alarming rate carelessly tossing aside any white fluffy clouds that got in their way. Within minutes the breeze that had been so prevalent throughout the day was replaced by an eerie calm. Except for the storm clouds above everything else was extremely still. We all knew based on the horror stories Mom had told us throughout the years that having a major calm before a storm was not good news.

Mom gathered us in her arms and prepared us to run the short distance from the door to the storm cellar. It was at just about that same time that the sky broke loose. Within an instant, we all knew it was too late to try to make it to the cellar. The storm was directly upon us. Instead or going to the cellar we huddled together and listened intently as the thunder roared and the lightening cracked. Then out of nowhere came the wind and the hail. Hail the size of golf balls and wind unlike we ever had felt before. The large branches on the old oak trees that stood so tall and majestic in our front yard were now almost touching the ground. It was as though the wind from the storm was making the tree bow and pay homage.

By this time we reached the house, my mother was practically hysterical. She was glaring at my father with a look that could of frozen boiling water. What we didn't' know at the time was that Dad , upon hearing Mom babbling on about how bad the upcoming storm was going to be, had confidently predicted that the storm would pass without incident. The cocky tone in his voice had emphasized that there would be no need to go to the basement. The heated discussion that had ensued between the two of them had caused the delay in calling us out of the haymow.

Now, as a result we were all too late to make our way to the cellar. Obviously, he had been wrong and now Mom was going to make sure he knew it. We were forced to just hunker down and ride out the storm in the porch of the house. The eerie calm was now gone; replaced instead by what sounded like a roaring freight train. Mom had always said that if a tornado was near the sound would be that of a freight train. She was right because it was at precisely that moment that we first saw the tornado funnel cloud. We were smack dab in the middle of a tornado.

Directly in its path was our tobacco shed. The tobacco shed is a large wooden structure about the size of the barn and is used to store tobacco in the fall and early winter. The tornado looked as though it was handling a delicate piece of china as it lifted the tobacco shed off its foundation. It picked up the entire structure, moved it about 20 feet and then set it back down. The only problem was that instead of setting it back on the foundation it was set directly on the gravel county road adjacent to our house. Then as though an afterthought the tail brushed the edge of the building and crash, it crumbled into thousands of pieces. It was as though we were in a slow motion scene from the Wizard of Oz. Debris was flying in every direction.

Then, just as quickly as the storm had started, it was over. The wind, the hail, the bluish-green-grey sky were gone. Once again an eerie calm returned to the air. The sky was now a mellow blue with fluffy white "whipped cream" clouds floating about. The temperature had dropped over twenty degrees in a matter of minutes and the rain had now slowed to just a trickle. Before Mom even realized what was going on Dad flew out of the house to survey the damage. She had had no chance to raise any type of objection.

Dad was gone for what seemed like an eternity. We saw him darting from one building to the next like a high school track star. He was spending the majority of his time in the buildings that housed animals. Suddenly we saw him running back towards the house. His arms were waving loudly and his lips were moving wildly. He was too far away for us to actually hear what he was saying. Mom ran out to meet him and it was only then we were finally able to hear what Dad was saying. He was shouting for help. One of our silo's had collapsed trapping several cows. Something had to be done.

For those of you who are not familiar with farm structures, a silo is a large circular structure usually made out of concrete blocks. It is used primarily to store silage. Silage is a special kind of feed made of hay and sometimes corn used to feed the farm animals. In our case the silo was approximately forty feet high and was supported with several metal rods.

The storm had practically shredded the concrete silo and as a result falling debris had trapped several cows and one bull. The animals were desperately trying to get out from under the debris but with no avail. The sound of the struggling animals was something that I will never forget. Once my dad finally reached the house he told us to immediately call the neighbors. He said to tell them what had happened and ask them to come as quickly as they could. We were told to remain in the house and stay put. My dad's voice was shaking and tears welled in his eyes. We had never seen my Dad so upset. Mom agreed that it was best for us kids to stay in the house and suggested that we turn on the television to help pass the time. We knew that something serious was going on because my Mom never allowed us to watch TV unless there was a special reason.

Even though we were young, we suddenly realized what needed to be done. The animals were injured and suffering. They needed to be put out of their misery. Thank goodness the neighbors came quickly. Mom and Dad's farm neighbors were the best. We could always count on them for help. This time was certainly no exception. One neighbor came carrying something in his arms. It was a case that was long, narrow and brown. We later learned that he had a gun and several rounds of ammunition inside the case. We heard a couple of very loud bangs and then nothing. In a matter of a few minutes we could no longer hear the animals struggling. While we were sad that the animals were dead, we were thankful that they were no longer suffering.

That evening all was quiet. The wind, the clouds and even the birds were still. Even though no one was really tired; everyone went to bed early and without any debate. The weather had taken its toll; our spirits were spent.

Shortly after midnight that very same night I was awakened to the sound of thunder erupting simultaneously with an intense bolt of lightning. Mom had taught us to count the time it took from the sound of thunder to when we saw lightening. She said the amount of time between the two meant how many seconds away the storm was from your location. Given what had just happened, thunder and lightning occurring at the same time, I knew the storm was directly upon us.

What happened next is forever engrained in my mind. There was yet another clap of thunder and crack of lightening occurring at the same time. This time lightening had directly struck the electrical box affixed to a tall pole just outside my bedroom window sending a bolt of electricity directly into my bedroom. The electrical surge exploded the light bulb in the ceiling of my bedroom and sent glass chars everywhere. There was so much electricity in the air that it caused my hair to stand on end. I was so stunned that all I could do was try to hide under my covers. Everything happened so fast that I don't think I even had a chance to scream.

The noise and commotion from the lightning strike and subsequent fire bolt woke up the entire house. Our bedrooms were all on the second floor and before I could call for help everyone was running toward my room to see what had happened. Dad was the first to enter my room and told everyone else to remain in the hallway. He was concerned about the broken glass and the potential for fire. He didn't want anyone going into my room for fear they might get hurt. He quickly put on a pair of shoes and carefully made his way to my bed. He reassured me that everything would be fine and then carried me out of my room into the hallway. It was then that we all realized how distressed my Mom was. She was beside herself. Dad did his best to comfort her and we all gave her our best hugs and kisses to assure her and us for that matter that everything was going to be ok.

As our family gathered in my room to assess the damage, the thunder and lightning subsided. Once again all was quiet. We cleaned up the broken glass from the light bulb, assessed the rest of the house for damage and concluded that all was well. No one had been hurt and the overall damage had been minimal but we were all very scared. We begged our parents to sleep downstairs to which they both agreed. Even though I think my father would have rather we all remained upstairs, he agreed without hesitation to have us all camp out in the living room for the rest of the night. It was in the log portion of the house. Mom had always told us that this portion of the house was the safest, sturdiest part of the house. That night it was just what we needed. Finally, in the safety of the log living room we all fell asleep.

Morning came quickly. Dad was up at his normal time, 4:30 AM to do his chores and then drive school bus. Our routine was normal as well. We woke to Mom's cheerful, "good morning sunshine's" and ran quickly upstairs to get ready for school. As I thumbed through my closet for something to wear an intensely bright yellow sun peeked through my pink gingham curtains. The sun seemed eager to block out last night's storm as though it had been a bad dream. The only real remnants of the storm were the puddles that littered the yard and the hint of an electrical charge that lingered in the air smelling a bit like smoke.

We were running late and had no time for breakfast. Mom was not pleased with our skipping breakfast but knew now was not the time to fuss over food. Instead she gave each of us a special hug before we jumped on our respective bikes and headed off for Clockmaker School. This by the way was the same school Mom had attended when she was a little girl. We rode our bikes at record speed and managed to arrive at school ten minutes before the first bell. Adrenaline from the night before must have still been in our systems fueling our quickened pace.

Shortly before noon, during Math class, we heard the fire alarm in the city of Westby sound. Westby was approximately three miles away from the farm. As was common in rural communities Westby had continued the tradition of sounding the siren at twelve o'clock every day. They did this to let people know it was lunch time. At first I assumed that the siren was sounding because it was twelve o'clock. When I glanced at the clock hanging in the front of the classroom however I realized it was only 11:50 AM. Everyone was talking. Something was not right. Everyone knew there must be a fire somewhere. The sirens grew louder and louder and the chatter of my classmates escalated. Several kids jumped up to look out the windows just as the fire trucks roared past our school. They were traveling fast up the county road in the direction of our farm. There were only five farms on our road. I sensed something was terribly wrong. Despite my best efforts, the pit in my stomach would not go away. Our teacher dismissed all the kids for lunch and recess. I decided to stay in my classroom. I was not so hungry. It was then that I overheard one of my classmate's say that the "Ekern" barn was on fire. He continued on, in a very nonchalant manner, to explain that the cows were even on fire.

The "Ekern" barn was on fire. The words played over and over again in my mind. Was this really true? My family's barn was burning to the ground. No, I thought, this could not possibly be happening! My teacher pulled up a chair next to my desk and did her best to make small talk with me. She was obviously trying to distract me from what I had just heard. The other teacher quickly escorted any remaining students out of the room and closed the door. After what seemed like a long time the other teacher returned to the classroom. This time she returned with my two brothers. She was holding their hands. As they approached me I noticed tears in not only the teacher's eyes but also in the eyes of my brothers. It was then that she confirmed what my heart already knew. It was now official. In deed our barn was burning. The building was fully engulfed in flames and many of our animals were trapped and would most certainly die. As bad as this news was, my most frightening moment came when I realized that my father was home alone.

My mother was at a church function helping to serve lunch for an afternoon funeral when she heard the siren. She too had felt an uneasy feeling that something was wrong. She tried to call my Dad from the church phone but no one had answered. By this point she was trembling and unable to drive. One of her friends drove her home only to see flames spanning the skyline as they drove up the ridge road. Unable to immediately locate Dad she began hysterically calling his name. Coughing, he came running from the backside of the barn and lifted her up off the ground. He carried her to the picnic table that sat in the shade of the big maple tree just outside the house and told her to stay put. He did his best to reassure that everything would be fine and then quickly returned to the burning building. She knew that things were not going to be fine; at least not for a very long time, but knew that now was not the time for a debate. Mom, now in shock, was unable to provide any meaningful assistance to Dad or the firefighters. All she could do was sit with her friend on the picnic bench and watch.

It was there that she watched Dad, a couple of neighbors and a team of firemen try to get animals out of the barn. The fire had started in the hay mow and had quickly spread to the entire building. Firemen thought that the lightning strike from the night before had traveled from the outside electrical wires into haymow where small fires smoldered for most of the night. The hay mow was relatively full at the time of the fire, containing roughly eight hundred hay bales and once enough oxygen combined with the smoldering embers the hay bales had literally blown up. This spontaneous combustion blew flames and debris in every direction causing immediate flames and fire in every inch of the barn. Most of the animals did not know what had hit them. Those that remained alive were confused and were struggling to survive. Despite the best efforts of the volunteer fire department, the flames continued to grow higher and hotter.

The animals that had been rescued were now instinctively trying to get back into the barn. Even the young stock animals that had been out in the pasture had gathered together and were trying their best to get into the barn. After all this was their home. The task of keeping them away from the barn proved to be both challenging and dangerous. Several firemen did their best to "shoo" them away and corral them but in the end they had to abandon the effort for the sake of helping to fight the actual fire. The fire now raging out of control was threatening to spread to some of the other buildings and possibly even the house. As a result, several once rescued animals including young stock perished in the fire.

The milking parlor contained a stainless steel bulk tank which was used for storing milk. It was a very expensive piece of equipment so Dad was eager to try to save it from the fire. The empty tank weighed approximately five hundred pounds. Dad and a person unknown to Dad or any of the firemen managed to carry the tank out of the burning building. After the fire Dad wanted the bulk tank moved to a storage building. He asked a neighbor to help him move it but they were unable to even budge the large object. This time it took six strong men to physically move the tank. Dad realized then how adrenaline can produce herculean strength. He also wandered who had helped him; it was then that he began to believe in the power of angels.

Back at school, our teacher decided it would be best if we did not immediately leave school and go to the fire. For this I was grateful. When the school day was finally over one of our teachers drove my brothers and me to our home. As we drove into the driveway, hot embers glowed and flames continued to shoot into the sky as firefighters continued to battle this blaze. It was obvious that the barn was a complete loss. The smell was overwhelming. Charred animals, burned wood, and the aroma of smoldering hay soaked with gallons of water filled the air. My father, soot filled and exhausted ran to greet us. He scooped us up in his arms and assured us that everything was going to be fine. My mother, still in a state of shock, said nothing. She just motioned us onto her lap and cradled and hugged us as we watched and listened to everything that was happening around us. For the first time in my life I was frightened. All we could do was sit there and stare at the devastation. Neighbors did their best to console us bringing food, refreshments and well wishes. As late afternoon faded and evening drew to a close even the sunset was muted. The heavy blanket of smoke and ash had consumed us all.

The pile of rubble that was once our barn continued to smolder for several days with hot spots flaring up from time to time. A portion of the fire department stayed at our farm for several days. The smell was the worst. It lingered and lingered serving as a constant reminder of the devastation that had occurred. My dad continued to sift through the rubble acting like a boy on Christmas morning with each little trinket he found that was salvageable. Mom barely existed. We longed for the carefree Mom and the playful relationship she and Dad shared. Things seemed so bleak. What in the world was our family going to do?

The insurance company was quick to do an assessment and confirmed that the fire was caused by lightning and would be covered by their policy. Apparently the lightening from the storm the night before had not only exploded the light bulb in my bedroom; but had also traveled along the power line into the hay mow. There the sparks smoldered for almost twelve hours before the flames ignited. They ruled the barn and its contents a total loss. This included compensation for the animals which perished in the fire. Unfortunately, the fine print of their policy said that the amount of compensation would be determined based on the original price of the structure not the current replacement value. So any hopes of watching their recently established savings account grow would now be out of the question.

As best he could, Dad submitted a list of the contents of the barn to the Insurance Company. In a matter of two weeks they received a sizable check in the mail. The amount was not enough to totally replace everything they had lost in the fire but it would go a long way toward helping them rebuild. The real problem facing Mom and Dad wasn't the amount of the money but what to do with the money. My parents strongly disagreed about how the money would be used.

Mom wanted to quit farming, take the insurance money, move to town and get a "regular 8-5 job." Dad wanted to rebuild the barn, buy more livestock and continue farming. They debated the topic at what seemed like every opportunity. Trying to remain objective, I would watch and listen and pray that this would soon all be behind us.

One night as I did the dishes I stretched my ears to listen as Mom and Dad once again banter about options. As I did this, I accidently dropped one of my Mom's favorite bowls. It was one of the few glass pieces that had been her mothers and it was priceless in her eyes. Before I knew what had happened it had slipped from my hands and now lay in pieces on the floor. I fell to the floor and burst into tears. Everything was falling apart; my mom's favorite dish was in pieces and so were our lives.

My carelessness was certainly going to upset both Mom and Dad; adding to the tension that was already consuming our house. I knew that I was going to be in big trouble for being so careless. Much to my surprise both my mom and dad ran to comfort me. They quickly reassured me that this had been just an accident and that everything would be fine. They both obviously sensed that my tears went well beyond breaking the bowl and decided at that moment that a decision had to be made regarding our families livelihood. While we could not fix the broken bowl or restore the barn, or bring back the animals but we certainly could and would find a way to go on.

Within a week decisions were made and progress was underway to rebuild our lives. Much to my pleasure my parents made the decision to rebuild and continue farming. I am sure that this was not my Mom's first choice but knew Dad would not be happy working in the city. She did of course love the homestead and knew that raising their children on this farm was in everyone's best interest. Once the decision was made the tension immediately evaporated from the house. Mom and Dad were busy discussing plans and a kind of hustle and bustle filled the air.

The neighbors were quick to help set up a make-shift barn in an old chicken coop where Dad could milk the cows that remained. To say that the conditions were poor would have been a total understatement. The building, only slightly larger than a single car garage, had no ventilation and could only handle four cows at a time. The cows had to be rotated from the pasture to the barn and vice versa in order to complete just one milking. The spring/early summer weather was extremely hot. With the additional heat generated from the cows the building became much more like a sauna than a milking parlor. During the time it took Dad to milk the cows, he could easily sweat off five pounds. In fact during the peak heat of the summer, he kept a garden hose nearby to provide instant relief should the heat become too overbearing.

Dad didn't complain even though it took him twice as long to milk the cows and even longer to do the rest of the daily chores. His hours now extended almost around the clock with no time for anything but farming and driving bus. Mom did her best to help out where she could; but given her slight stature she did not have the physical strength to do a lot of the farm work. Plus, caring for the house, garden and the three of us kids consumed most of her waking hours.

The good news was that school would soon be out and Dad would have the summer to rebuild the barn. Dad had decided to build the barn himself given their limited funds. Mom wanted to hire someone to at least be the general contractor for the project but knew that was out of the question. Dad had assured her that somehow he would find a way to manage both building the barn and taking care of the large amount of field work that the summer season required. He was a very determined individual and Mom knew that once he put his mind to something there was no stopping him. A little stubborn streak he had perhaps inherited from his mother Martha.

Anyway, as I mentioned earlier Dad epitomized the term jack-of-all trades. Self-taught in almost every regard, I do not recall any skill that my Dad could not do. As we experienced firsthand that summer his energy and can-do attitude served as an inspiration to anyone that he came in contact with. He had decided that rather than rebuild the barn in the original style, the typical red-all-wood structure, he was going to do something different. He had studied farm magazines, consulted with various suppliers at the feed mill and visited several construction sites before coming up with his final design. He never used blueprints or any architectural drawings for that matter, instead relying on pencil scribbles and sketches on everything from scrap pieces of paper to old scraps of wood.   For the most part though, the plan was in his head. He had mentally created exactly what he wanted and was now faced with the task of actually building it. He knew in general what he was going to construct, the dimensions and type of materials, and believed that everything else, like the rest of the details, could be determined as construction took place. In addition to his normal summer farming demands, he was now going to be general contractor, chief carpenter, mason, electrician, plumber, painter and crew foreman.

Once Mom and Dad had made the final decision to rebuild, a friend who does excavating for a living came to them with an idea. He offered to dig a large pit and bury all the debris that remained from the fire. He said that he would dig the hole several hundred yards from the burn site, bulldoze the remains into the pit and then cover both areas with top soil. All of this he would do free of charge. Mom and Dad were thrilled with the idea and extremely grateful for his generosity. The very next day he and his crew arrived at the farm and went to work. The location of the pit quickly became the graveyard for the debris and a resting place for the cattle and other farm animals that had perished in the fire. The sound of the earthmovers moaning and shaking as they pushed and maneuvered every last spec of debris was surreal. One day a pile of rubble and the next a clear plot ready to rebuild a fresh future.

A New Beginning

Dad was eager to begin construction so as soon as the excavating crew left he began to stake out the quadrants for the new barn. The new barn would be majorly different from the original 100 year old barn constructed on approximately the same site. Dad's plan for the barn would include a concrete block foundation with a rounded wooden roof. Included in the barn would be stalls for fifty cows, twenty-five on each side plus on the west end there would be calf pens. On the east end there would be direct access to the silo and an automated barn cleaner. Adjacent to the barn would be a milk house where the milk would be stored in the bulk tank. It was to be a sanitized area with a huge glass picture window looking into the barn. The entire project would no doubt require the very best of Dad's skills.

The concrete blocks used for the foundation would need to be meticulously placed and cemented. The rafters needed for the roof would require precision measurement and careful construction. The most difficult part of the entire process however would involve the placement of the pre-made rafters onto the concrete foundation. Figuring out how to hoist the large wooden rafters and then fasten them to the foundation remained a mystery to Dad. While he had tossed and turned various ideas on how to accomplish, he had yet to determine the best approach to take. Instead of spending too much more time thinking on this matter he decided to put this "detail" off until the time came to actually raise the rafters. He was certain that once he could physically see all the components he would be able to figure out the best way to proceed.

Very early in their decision to rebuild, Dad realized he was going to need a great deal of help if he was going to finish the barn before the new school year started. Not only would he need help for the barn construction but he would also need help for planting and tending to the crops. He had one summer, exactly nine weeks in which to construct the barn. This is where he first began to really rely on the kids of Bus Number 7. Since the time of the fire parents and family members of Bus Number 7 kids had offered their support in the form of homemade meals and the promise of access to manpower. Many of the families on Dad's route had high school age boys that were physically very strong and used to the hard work. Dad decided to take them up on their offers. He was hopeful that many of the boys would be willing to work for him on the farm for the summer. During the last week of school he made an unscheduled stop. Just before delivering his bus load of kids to school, he pulled onto the shoulder of the road and announced that he was looking for summer help. He continued this process for the next five days making sure that everyone heard the message. Loud and clear, he was looking for boys, yes girls were welcome too, to not only help with the building of the barn but also to care for cattle, milk cows and tend to crops.

The response to Dad's request for summer help was overwhelming. Dad's offer to fairly compensate these youngsters with weekly pay, meals and transportation if needed was more than most of the kids had ever been exposed to. Several of the families now faced a tough choice. While they needed the help of their own kids on their farms, they also wanted to do what they could to help Dad and realized that this was a unique chance for their children to both learn some new skills but also make some extra income. By the end of the school year fifteen boys ranging in ages from thirteen to nineteen had signed on to work with Dad for the summer. Three of the oldest boys had their driver's license and agreed to provide the rest of the boy's transportation to and from the farm each day. Since all the boys lived a short distance from each other the parents of the two oldest boys offered their vehicles free of charge for this service as their way of showing Mom and Dad their support. The summer was certainly going to be a learning experience for not only Dad but also the young boys.

One of the boys that agreed to help had been a bit of a trouble maker on Dad's bus. He was from a large family and had a knack for pestering and teasing anyone in his presence; especially the girls. He was a rather immature blonde boy who was always demanding Dad's attention. He had so much energy that at times he seemed almost unable to contain himself. He never did anything really bad, but was always someone who Dad had to keep in his rearview mirror. This distinction had earned him a place on the bus directly behind him. The first seat behind Dad's driver's seat was always reserved for this boy. Several of the veteran drivers during early morning coffee at the bus garage one morning had mentioned that having problem children sit directly behind them had gone a long way to curb any troublesome behavior. That very same day Dad had tried this out on this boy and was happy to report back to his fellow drivers that it had in fact worked. This was a technique that he wound up using for as long as he drove bus. Keeping any problem children in the seat directly behind him dramatically reduced behavior problems and equally important if not more important had dramatically reduced the stress level for Dad. Even though Dad had had numerous bouts with this boy throughout the last year, he agreed to hire him just the same. He was sure that his unending source of energy would be a great asset. Dad also hired a couple of this boy's brothers and knew that if push came to shove; he could always have a little "brotherly" pressure" applied if necessary.

During the last week of school Dad and met with his new "helpers" and outlined what they would be doing that summer. Three oldest most experienced farm machinery boys were put in charge of tending to the crops and doing barn chores. The rest of the boys would be Dad's construction crew. None of the construction crew boys had any previous experience in construction, but that didn't bother Dad. He was confident that he would be able to teach them everything they would need to know and that by the end of the summer together they would have constructed a barn.

Dad had the concrete blocks, pallets of wood and miscellaneous supplies delivered to the farm just in time for the first week of summer vacation. His Bus Number 7 crew arrived promptly at 7 am the day after school ended. He had mentally created a timeline of tasks to be completed during the first week and immediately assigned tasks to the boys upon their arrival. Dad had staked out and leveled the ground prior the boys arriving so the first significant job was hand mixing cement and beginning to form the block foundation. This was heavy laborious work.

Hand mixing cement meant taking great care to mix the exact amounts of water, dry cement, and sand in order to achieve the texture necessary to form a solid foundation. Dad entrusted this task to one of his senior kids and was extremely pleased by his attention to detail and focus. His efforts were flawless. The three boys charged with carrying and delivering the dry bags of cement and keeping the sand pile adequately stocked to make sure that there were always supplies available for the hand mixer who worked tirelessly from morning until day's end.

Several of the younger boys were responsible for transporting the cement from the hand mixer to the foundation site using a couple of wheel barrels. Although well intended; their efforts were less than flawless. Maneuvering a three wheeled cart loaded to the brim with wet cement was no easy task. It required concentration and strength; neither of which the boys assigned to this task possessed. Dad decided to have the wheel barrels loaded only half full and created a game out of who could deliver the most loads without a spill. This small change dramatically improved results. The challenge increased both their speed and their accuracy. The boys decided to form teams and made a contest out of which team could deliver the most loads without a spill. The boys decided that the prize for winning would be that the losing team would have to get them drinking water from the well whenever they wanted it for one entire week.

Dad watched in delight as the boys giggled, cheered and carried on. He was amazed by how creative they had become. They were constantly trying faster and better ways to transport the loads of wet concrete without spilling a drop. The spirit of competition was certainly producing favorable results.

While the boys were responsible for making and transporting the concrete, Dad did the actual laying of the concrete blocks. Mason work required meticulous attention to detail. This was after all going to be the foundation for the entire barn. It was imperative that the blocks be placed and cemented in place using exact measurements. A crooked foundation meant a crooked barn. It was during this time that Dad began to use the phrase, "measure once, measure again, and then lay". Throughout the years he would become known for using the measure once, measure again philosophy. You see in the case of the barn, having the foundation be off even by a couple of inches on either side would easily produce an upper story or a roof that could be off by more than a foot. Dad knew that by giving extra time and attention to the placement of the foundation it would make the entire job easier. While a little discouraged by how slow the work of laying the actual block was progressing he was delighted by the efforts of his young crew. By the end of the first week the boys had mastered their respective jobs and seemed genuinely pleased by their accomplishments.

Once the foundation was complete the crew turned their attention to building a platform on top of the concrete blocks. This was to be the ceiling for the barn and the floor of the hay mow. This job involved nailing rows and rows of boards to 2 x 4 studs that had been anchored to the top of the foundation. All the boys regardless of age seemed to enjoy this task. The job of carrying and nailing each board in place went quickly and they reveled at how fast they were able to complete this project. This personally was my favorite part of the entire barn project. The smell of the wood permeated the air and the sun reflected brightly from what became to look almost like a basketball court. Even though this "court" was approximately twelve feet in the air it was none the less still a smooth even surface that welcomed the wild and crazy antics from the boys. From cartwheels, to playing catch, to playing tag, the surface provided a place to do it all.

It was during this time that I developed a crush on one of the older boys. He was blond, tan, and had the most beautiful blue eyes that I have ever seen. I made it my job to hand him nails. That's right, I spent several entire days at his side handing him nail after nail focusing on his hand gestures to know just the right moment to hand him another nail. Sometimes I even touched his hand! At the age of eight, I must have looked like a total fool, but I didn't care. I took great pride in my job and was able to easily disregard the teasing that ensued for my behavior. After all I had two brothers and was used to constant teasing and heckling.

By this time it was several weeks into the summer and the newness and novelty of working construction was beginning to wane. The work was hard and the days were extremely long. They worked from seven am to seven pm, Monday through Thursday. On Friday and Saturday they worked until only five pm which to most of them seemed like a huge bonus. Dad had also decided there would be no work on Sunday which proved to be a very positive decision. Not only did this give the boys a little time for themselves or to be with their families, it also gave Dad a chance to regroup and make sure he had enough supplies and jobs in mind to keep everyone busy for the upcoming week. We would go to church on Sunday morning and enjoy a big noon meal. If Dad was lucky he would take an afternoon nap. This summer had not afforded him any thirty minute after lunch naps; so Sunday afternoon provided him a rare chance to catch up on a little bit of rest and do something for himself.

The next major construction task was to build the rafters for the roof. As Dad had known, the design would be challenging as the rafters were rounded and required just the right angles in order to create the right roof pitch. Dad's plan was to prebuild twenty-five rafters. They would be constructed on the ground using large nail spikes. After they were built they would be hoisted on top of the foundation and nailed in place. Although he had not yet figured out how he was going to raise the rafters to the foundation he mentally decided that he had plenty of mental time to figure this out and for now the top priority was to prebuild the rafters. Throughout the construction of the barn and during any other major project in Dad's life he used his mental skills to determine when and how to do something and was known to take "time outs" to think about what his next steps would be.

After about two days of pounding spikes into the rafters Dad learned that one of the shyest boys in the entire crew had blisters, the size of quarters covering his fingers and the palms of his hands. You have to remember that all the carpentry work was done with an old fashioned hammer. There were no electric nail guns or power tools to help pound the nails or screws. This meant that the entire structure was hand nailed using a heavy hammer and four inch spikes. The boy had tried hard to keep his hands covered but during lunch break one of the other boys had noticed the blisters and casually mentioned it to Dad. Dad took the boy aside and couldn't believe how the boy was able to keep working given the size and intensity of his blisters. Dad told him to take a few days off in order to give their blisters a chance to heal. The boy refused however insisting that they were really not all that painful. Dad himself had more than his share of blisters over the years and knew one thing was for sure; they were painful.

The boy kept reassuring him that his work would not suffer because of the blisters. He continued to show up each and every day without once complaining. In fact he was so intent on living up to Dad's standards that one day he showed up with a mallet instead of a hammer and bandages on all his fingers. He was determined that despite the blisters he could continue to be productive. Dad was extremely impressed by this youngster's work ethic and determination. It was just about that time when Dad learned that the boy's father had died at an early age and as a result had never had a father figure for which to confide in. As the summer progressed, this youngster became Dad's right hand man. In fact as the years progressed he became one of Dad's dearest friends.

The time had finally arrived to raise the rafters onto the top of the twelve foot high concrete foundation. The last of the prebuilt rafters was complete and now lay neatly stacked awaiting this process. The time had come for Dad to announce how he planned to accomplish this feat. He had received plenty of input from neighbors and friends but in the end opted for the method suggested by one of his Bus #7 crew. One of the more intellectual boys in the crew had suggested a pulley system anchored by large scaffolding. Once they were individually hoisted to the roof they would use tractors, one on each end of the barn, several ropes and a crew of twenty men to manually move the rafters into place. Dad mentally worked and reworked this idea until he was confident it was the right answer.

While there were a couple of minor adjusts needed the day of the big event, mostly in the tension of the ropes, the rafters were placed on the roof with little to no problem. Much to the surprise of onlookers who were skeptical of Dad's methods, by day's end half of the rafters were in place. The next day proved equally as successful resulting in all the rafters in place and semi-secured. It would take several days before they would be 100% secured and anchored. We all prayed for good weather and especially asked that the wind remain calm since any significant gusts could easily topple the rafters much like the game of dominos. It was a high stakes proposition. Dad and his entire Bus #7 crew worked from sunrise to sunset during this time in order to take advantage of the favorable weather. As a reward for all the hard work and success in raising the rafters, dad gave the entire crew two days off.

With a couple of days rest under their belts the crew returned to begin the task of roofing the barn. Given the height and pitch of the roof this proved to be a difficult task; one that Dad quite honestly had not given a lot of thought to. Mom had been the first one to point out this fact as she watched from the ground as the final rafters had been moved into place. Mom was the worry wart in the family. She was always on the lookout for impending danger zones when it came to her kids, or the kids of Bus Number 7 she was very protective. While Dad at times would dismiss her concerns as that of an overly protective mother, Dad too realized that the roof did present a potential hazard. Once he understood this, he decided they would need to build and use scaffolding on the entire roof. He also decided that harnesses would be used when they worked on the highest sections of the barn. This would be mandatory. Dad was extremely concerned about the safety of his crew and made sure that everyone knew the rules. He was extremely relieved when the highest section of the roof was finally complete.

Roofing the lower section of the barn would be much safer, Dad had reassured Mom. They would need to use only scaffolding and ladders for the lower section. Just as they were about to finish the last portion of the lower section, Dad's scaffolding broke. Before anyone had a chance to say a word, his body and pieces of the scaffolding went tumbling to the ground. There was Dad wearing only cut-off jean shorts and work boots; lying flat on the ground. He was quick to assure everyone that he was fine, but one quick look in the direction of his leg everyone knew that this was not the case.

The direction of his foot relative to his leg told the real story. Dad's ankle was badly broken. It was broken so badly in fact that his foot was actually pointing in the wrong direction. The pain must have been intense, however Dad never let on that this was the case. He never complained about the pain, but certainly made it known that he was not happy about having to miss a couple hours of good daylight in order to go to the emergency room. The emergency room was approximately ten miles from the farm. Mom was not home at the time of the accident so one of the oldest boys drove him to the hospital.

Within a matter of a few hours he was back from the hospital's emergency room. X-rays revealed that several bones in his right ankle were in fact broken. The doctor proceeded to reset the bones and cast his leg. The hard cast went from the tips of his toes to just below his knee. The breaks had been clean and therefore did not require any surgery. Fortunate the doctor had commented; although fortunate was not the word Dad would have used to describe the situation. He had just over a month until school would once again begin and there was a great deal of work left to be done before the barn would be complete. In addition he wasn't sure how he was going to be able to drive the bus given his hard cast. Rather than spend too much time dwelling on all the things he couldn't change Dad decided to do his best to take this whole matter in stride.

Mom was still not home yet when they returned from the hospital. You can imagine her shock as she drove into the driveway and saw Dad, crutches in tow, standing next to the crumbled scaffolding. Dad dropped what he was doing and proceeded to hobble toward her waving his crutches in the air as though some sort of sign of reassurance. She was not amused running to meet him. Dad hugged her, proceeded to tell her what had happened and assured her that everything would be fine. He downplayed the accident and told her that the Doctor had not given him any limitations, except that he not climb on a ladder for a couple of days. Mom wasn't sure she totally believed him but given Dad's nature, she knew that she was not going to be able to really do anything to slow him down.

Although he wasn't able to climb for a couple of days, he continued to provide supervision to his crew and even milked the cows that evening. Mom had offered to help but Dad had insisted he was fine. You see Mom had, early on in their farming career, been kicked by a cow. She had landed on her tailbone and as a result had frequent back aches and pain. Dad was not about to let her risk any future chance of injury. He preferred she stay out of the barn and tonight would be no different. He had however accepted the offer by two of his Bus #7 kids to finish the farm chores which allowed Dad to finish his work about an hour earlier than normal.

The weeks that followed were filled with constructing the interior of the barn as well as installing the barn cleaner and pneumatic milking system. Throughout this time Dad's physical mobility remained limited. The injury was proving more challenging than he had first thought but he was not about to give up. The boys sensed his frustration and decided to construct a look-out bench, complete with a padded seat and a foot rest. This allowed Dad to continue to supervise without constantly being on his feet. He continued to turn over more and more responsibility to his Bus Number 7 crew and was delighted to see how they had risen to the occasion. They had even eagerly accepted the technically challenging task of installing the pneumatic milking system. With one kid reading the instructions aloud as several others assembled the multitude of pieces; they were pleasantly surprised when within a week they had it installed and working like a charm.

The barn building summer had been a growing experience not only for Dad but also for his Bus Number 7 crew. They had proven to be outstanding workers. They had met and exceeded Dad's expectations and were not only instrumental in the completion of the barn but also in keeping Dad's spirits high. Just as Dad had counted on each and every one of them to help build the barn, he also now realized how much they relied on him. I am sure there must have been periods of frustration and off-colored words, but I never heard Dad express either one. The lessons learned that summer went far beyond what could ever be taught in a classroom. By the end of the summer the barn was ready to carry on its intended function. Cows, calves, cats, barn swallows and other stray critters were enjoying their new surroundings and Mom and Dad could not have been happier.

And so it was as quickly the summer had started it was now over. It was time to once again gear up for another school year. Although not overly eager to resume another year of driving Bus Number 7 he knew this year would be different on several fronts. First of all Dad knew he would no longer have trouble with his immature little blonde boy. He had grown and matured a great deal in the months he had worked for Dad. He also knew that if there was any hint of trouble all he had to do was give him that certain special look and he would settle down. The young boy who once gave Dad and the girls on the bus a difficult time no longer had a pre assigned seat directly behind him on the bus. He had earned the right to freely choose where he would sit. It was interesting to Dad however that most days he chose to sit right behind Dad chatting non-stop from the time he was picked up until the time he was dropped off both to and from school.

Secondly, Dad became a mentor for the shy boy that had lost his father at a young age. Dad took him under his wing and did everything in his power to help him if he needed something. He routinely double checked his homework, gave advice on what sports to try out for and what to wear for his first school dance. Dad could see the boy's confidence growing as the year went on and was delighted when he asked Dad to come and watch his very first basketball game. Dad, himself a high school basketball player jumped at the chance and routinely went to each and every game that year.

Finally, Dad knew his relationship with the rest of the boys from his crew would be different than it had been in the past. The mutual respect and dignity they shared with each other was contagious. The atmosphere on the bus was more casual, giving way to more chatter and a great deal of laughter. Dad became more relaxed and actually started to look forward to driving the kids to and from school. He even agreed to give up his country music radio station for a "rock" station during the morning run. The evening run was his to choose, but knowing my Dad and his love for country music, it says a great deal about his interest in the bus kids to let them have their music for at least part of the route.

The bond that Dad and his summer buddies established would last for years; not only for their generation but also for future generations of their families. They valued Dad's input and relied on his counsel. Dad became their biggest fan cheering them on whether in sports, music, academics or life in general. Some fifty years later several of these boys continued to rely on dad for advice or to just hang out and reminisce about old times.

The year proved to be a pretty good one for driving bus. It marked a shift in Dad's driving purely out of necessity to one of driving at least some of the time out of pleasure. Dad no longer dreaded the interruption driving school bus caused in his farming day; but now found he was actually looking forward to spending some time with his kids.

I recall getting to go with him periodically for the evening run and was delighted when some of the older girls would let me sit with them and share grown-up girl stories. They even shared their "juicy fruit" gum with me. The best part of the trip however was the ride back into town once we had dropped off the last kid. Dad would let me sit in the way back seat of the bus. He would kick up his country western music especially loud making sure that I could hear it and then we would sail across the hills of

Lovaas Ridge. By this time Dad knew the route like the back of his hand and he had mastered the art of driving on the narrow gravel roads. He would accelerate just as we were going over the crest of the hills sending my stomach into my throat and my body bouncing at least a foot off the seat. Hands firmly clenched on the back of the seat in front of me I would call out to Dad to see if he could do it again. He would give me a quick wave and I could see by the look on his face, eyes gleaming at me through the rear view mirror, that he was about to give me yet another jolt. Then just as I was getting used to his technique we were coming to a stop and about to enter the city limits. It was time to get serious. No more games to be played, at least for this trip.

The years passed and Dad's fondness for driving continued to grow. The kids he had picked up on their first day of kindergarten were now graduating from high school. He had grown to know many of the kids as though they were his own. In addition to the basics like knowing names, ages, parent occupations, he had grown to know each one of them as only someone who has spent the better part of twelve years with someone can know. He was sometimes a counselor, sometimes a referee, sometimes a coach, a teacher and a friend; Dad's scope seemed to grow with each year that passed. Each summer he would hire a couple of his older Bus Number 7 kids to help out on the farm. While a number of the kids were siblings of the original crew, he made sure to include any new kids in the area or those that might be shy or have self-esteem issues.

The kids and families of Bus Number 7 now counted on Dad both during the school year as well as during the summer months. In addition to farming he took on roofing jobs during the summer months to help supplement the family income. Each summer he hired kids from his bus route to help him do this work. They roofed houses, barns, machine sheds and even a church or two. Dad loved teaching his kids the fine points of roofing and treasured the time they spent together. He became the sought after summer employer.

A Switch in Career and Focus

The years passed and in 1967 my youngest brother Todd was born. My two brothers and I were now in our teens and very busy with school activities. Dad missed being able to be more involved as a father in our lives and began to resent the demands dairy farming placed on his time. Mom had long thought dairy farming was too much work but had given up on the idea of trying to convince Dad to try something new. You can imagine her surprise when Dad approached her with the idea of switching from dairy farming to hog farming. Mom was all ears. Dad explained that hog farming was much less demanding, at least from a time standpoint, than dairy farming. While you had to feed and tend to the pigs, there was not the rigor and twice daily milking that dairy cows required.

Together they researched the pros and cons of hog farming and decided to focus on raising "feeder pigs". Feeder pigs is an industry term which means raising baby pigs until they weigh about fifty or sixty pounds and then selling them on the open market to other farmers who raise them for another two to three months or until they weigh around 250 pounds. It is at that time they are sold to the market for slaughter. The switch would require a sizeable investment and a degree of risk but both were eager to give it a try. The investment would include purchasing 200 sows, female pigs, and two boars, male pigs. They would convert the dairy barn to a hog facility and construct another building to accommodate all the animals. The final investment would be in the feed and nutrients, primarily corn and soy products and medications such as antibiotics. The risks were similar to any type of farming. The risk of crop failure, animal illness and disease were always present; but the biggest unknown was how much they would be paid for the animals at the time of sale. The realities of supply and demand would control in great part how much income they could actually generate. This time, pork would be their source of income verses milk when they were dairy farming.

Without too much debate, they decided to sell all the dairy livestock and get on about the business of hog farming. They both felt good about this decision especially knowing that they could count on Dad's bus driving job to provide additional income and most importantly health insurance for the family. The transition from dairy farming to hog farming was not as easy as Dad had first thought it would be. They purchased the animals and were surprised to find the sows did not become pregnant as soon as Dad had expected. Apparently the hogs, both male and female needed a period of adjustment to their new surroundings before breeding. Whatever the case, Dad ended up having to have the sows artificially inseminated which proved to be quite expensive. The delay in breeding meant that six months passed before they were able to generate any income from the pigs. The extra income from bus driving once again saved the day allowing them to just barely get by.

Once the sows started to give birth, which is called farrowing, Dad realized that the birthing process was not going to be quite as easy as it had been with cattle. Some of the sows would become quite violent when giving birth foaming at the mouth and trying to eat the newly born piglets. Each sow weighed about five hundred pounds could easily deliver ten to fifteen piglets within several minutes so Dad realized that having them in special farrowing crates was not going to be an option as he had once thought. He also realized that by feeding the sows a can of beer just as they were about to give birth did wonders to help relax the anxious soon-to-be-mothers. He also carried a hammer in his back pocket in the event that a sow decided to take out their frustration on Dad. A careful smack to the side of the head of one of the angry sows immediately brought them back in line. Once the initial kinks were worked out, Dad was pleased to find that the actual work required to tend to the hogs was significantly less than with the dairy cattle. He found the work much less demanding and was delighted with his increased flexibility.

The school system was always in need of bus drivers for extra-curricular activities and Dad's new schedule made it possible for him to accept some of these trips. His favorite was driving the football players and coaches for away games. He loved his football trips. Westby had an exceptionally strong football program which meant the pressure to win was strong and small town rivalries drew hundreds of people. Many of his own Bus Number 7 high school boys played football so Dad was thrilled to be able to spend more time with his boys. Now he was able to not only watch the games but also could listen in on what the coaches were telling the boys both before and after the games. Dad was quite the sideline coach and became an avid fan of the team. He was especially proud of his bus kids. Since many of the boys came from dairy farms, their parents were not able to attend many games. Dad took on a very important role in their lives. To and from school each week Dad and his players would rehash old games and anticipate upcoming games.

During Dad's third season of driving the football team, he was thrilled to learn that the varsity team had specifically requested him to be their driver for all the games. In addition to Dad having a personal relationship with many of the boys, the coaches also liked the fact that Dad was extremely punctual, he always knew the exact route he was going to take, (no getting lost or wasting time asking for directions) and he would eagerly take the team for a post-game meal or treat if requested. Dad was delighted with this request and eagerly accepted. Each and every game Dad would put on all his Westby school color paraphernalia and skillfully maneuver the big yellow bus carrying the varsity players and coaches. During the game he would pace up and down the sidelines like a proud father calling out words of encouragement and loads of advice. Half time meant that the team and coaches would return to the bus for their "pep" talk. Dad made sure that the bus was ready for them when they arrived; cool if the weather outside was hot muggy and warm if the season had suddenly turned cold and damp. He guarded the entrance of the bus as though the team's plays and strategies were somehow hidden deep within.

The football team would go undefeated that year; winning their final game of the season in overtime. The game was in DeSoto which is a small town along the river known for its especially tough farm kids of Italian decent. They too were undefeated so for both teams a great deal was at stake. The weather had turned unseasonably cold and on the evening of the game there were snow flurries in the air. The weather coupled with the intensity of the competition made conditions very difficult. Dad did his best to reduce the tension during the bus ride to DeSoto offering to give up his usual country western music. As the players boarded the bus, he told them they would be able to listen to the radio station of their choice, both going and returning. This gesture proved fruitless however when the head coach quickly proclaimed that there would be no music before the game. There was to be complete silence on the way to the game with each player meditating and focusing on the game ahead. Dad respected the coach's decision and actually appreciated the silence. The icy conditions and blowing snow flurries were going to make the forty-five minute winding trip from Westby's ridgetop location to Desoto's river bottom location challenging.

By the end of the first half the snow flurries had turned into sleet. The conditions on the field were very slippery and visibility was poor. Despite the best efforts of both teams, the game remained scoreless. Dad moved the bus as close as he could to the field and cranked up the heat so that the players and coaches could maximize their face time during the half-time discussion. Dad remained on the bus that night and listened as the coach adjusted and reinforced their second half strategy. Dad patted each player on the back as they left the bus to return to the field for the second half and gave an extra couple of pats to each coach. With seconds to go in the game both teams were frustrated with their inability to score. Westby however was in field goal range and one of Dad's "kids" was about to attempt the game winning kick. Dad moved to the end zone and watched as the center snapped the ball. The kick was low and slightly to the right, but somehow managed to just clear the goal posts. Players, coaches and fans rushed the end zone and before Dad knew it he was in the center of the celebration. His "kid" had scored the winning points. Dad raised the young man high in his arms as everyone cheered and yelled.

As the players and coaches boarded the bus for the return trip to Westby, there was no need for music. The noise level on the bus was out of control but Dad did not mind. As he carefully maneuvered the big yellow bus up and down the slippery roads he glanced into his rear view mirror and was amazed to see the string of cars that was behind his bus. The fans had decided to follow the player bus back to school and the result was something that looked like an old fashioned snake dance with Dad and his bus load of precious cargo leading the pack.

Roughly five miles outside of Westby, Dad's bus was greeted by the Westby fire and police department. They had heard of the big win and decided an escort was in order. The caravan slowly made its way to town with lights flashing and sirens blaring. Pride swelled within Dad as he drove the bus into Westby and parked in front of the gymnasium. He had safely delivered the team home for what would become one of the biggest post game rallies in Westby history. Everyone, players and fans alike packed the gymnasium where cheerleaders led the group celebrating the win. Dad joined the team and coaches at center court where a loud round of "hip, hip hooray" echoed through the corridors of the school. This was a night Dad would not soon forget and in fact he talked about this evening for years to come.

Mom and Dad continued to hog farm until roughly 1984 when disease struck the main barn killing several hundred feeder pigs. This coupled with depressed pork prices made their decision to quit farming quite easy. They sold the remaining hogs, auctioned off the farm equipment and put the farm up for sale. The farm sold quickly and within a couple of months they purchased a house in Westby and moved to town.

Leaving the Farm for City Life

They purchased a two story hundred year old house with a large yard. Mom loved the front porch complete with a swing and was sure that once they did a little remodeling work, the house would be perfect. Mom you see was always coming up with design ideas and ways to remodel and improve where they lived. During their time on the farm she had redesigned the main living area three times. Their move to town would be no different. Dad carefully listened to her design ideas and then skillfully and patiently went on about creating the living space she had envisioned. They were a good team, creating a lovely home for which to start this new phase in their lives.

One of the things they especially liked about this house was that it was on the Syttende Mai parade route. Each year on the Saturday nearest May 17th, Westby celebrated Norwegian Independence Day, known as Syttende Mai. Family, friends and many of Dad's bus kids and families would gather on the lawn to watch the parade. The swing on the front porch provided an excellent vantage point for observing the floats and bands. The first year that they lived in the house, the Westby High School band stopped directly in front of the house, turned to face them and played a song for Dad. Dad was speechless. The drum majorette, a bus rider of Dad's ran up and gave him a big hug whispering to him that the hug was from the entire band. This began a tradition with the band repeating this gesture in future years.

One of the other benefits of living where they did was the proximity to the high school and the bus garage; the garage was less than a half mile from their house. Dad took advantage of an alternative path to the bus garage during return trips from his route. Rather than go the normal route through town to the garage, he took the side street passing directly in front of their house honking as he went by. This became his signal to Mom that he would be home in twenty minutes. Time for him to park the bus, chat with fellow drivers and head home. This became Mom's way of knowing if he was having trouble on his route or if he was being delayed.

In addition to driving school bus Dad decided to get into the basement waterproofing business. The investment was minimal but the work was physically taxing. It involved drilling concrete and removing mud and cement from wet basements before installing sump pumps and other water deflecting devices. Again he enlisted the summer help of his bus kids. This time however the promise of returning to high school from summer vacation with a stellar tan from hours of roofing gave way instead to the not so glamorous task of spending hours a day in wet, many times moldy, basements shoveling mud and concrete. Dad found recruiting summer help more challenging but quickly offset the change in conditions with higher pay.

Much to both Mom and Dad's delight the waterproofing business became very successful. Dad's reputation for quality work and 100% satisfaction guarantee drew customers from several counties. Word of mouth provided him lead after lead. Within a couple of years the business was making more money than they had ever dreamed possible. It was the perfect complement to bus driving. Most of the waterproofing work was done during the late spring, summer, and early fall months which coincided with his bus driving schedule.

School bus driving was now a no brainer for Dad. Skillfully maneuvering the big yellow passenger bus through the winding picturesque ridges and coulees, he became known for his speed and accuracy. With ease and familiarity he knew every inch of his route like the back of his hand. He had also established himself as a no-nonsense driver, meaning that he expected his kids to behave in certain ways including treating each other with dignity and respect. Failure to comply with the bus rules would most certainly lead to consequences. On one occasion a junior high boy refused to listen to Dad when he told the boy to stop taunting an underclassman. Dad explained that if he didn't stop he would going to stop the bus and the boy would have to walk home. The boy called Dad's bluff continuing to taunt the underclassman. Much to the boys surprise as well as the other kids on the bus, he pulled the bus to the side of the road, stopped the engine, opened the door, and told the trouble maker to get off the bus. Dad told the boy he would be calling his parents to tell them that their son would be home late that day as he was walking home. The boy, realizing that Dad was serious, quickly apologized to both Dad and the classmate he had been taunting and promised to never again cause any trouble. After several, what must have been long minutes to the trouble maker, Dad restarted the bus and resumed the route. A lesson was learned by not only the trouble maker but by the rest of the kids on the bus.

Most of the bus drivers in the Westby School district were retired farmers. As they gathered each morning at the bus garage to check over their buses and prepare for the morning run, they told jokes, expressed political views and chit-chatted about everything under the sun. They became a close bunch sharing fresh brewed coffee and homemade treats each morning. Their coffee clutch was a great way to start the day and became a valued part of Dad's bus driving experience.

After years of driving school bus Dad was surprised to learn that he was being presented with a special award. The State of Wisconsin was recognizing him for his years of service and his outstanding driving record. The State of Wisconsin had never had anyone drive school bus as many years as Dad had driven. Equally impressive was the fact that Dad had never had an accident. The school administrator called a special meeting of all the bus drivers after the evening route and gave a short speech as he acknowledged Dad's unique contribution. He was one of only several in the state to ever have achieved such a reward. Dad eagerly accepted the award, but was quick to down play the importance of his accomplishment. He was after all, just doing his job.

Good thing for Dad that he had not let his award go to his head because only two short weeks after receiving this honor he had his first bus accident. He had arrived at the bus garage early that morning and having completed his pre-route inspection spent a little extra time conversing with his fellow drivers. Before he knew it he was running a little late and without thinking jumped onto his seat, started the engine and proceeded to back up the bus. Clunk…the noise was deafening. Dad in his haste had failed to open the garage door. He slammed on the brakes and jumped out of the bus to inspect the damage. Much to his dismay, many of his fellow drivers had already congregated outside the garage to see what had caused the commotion. While Dad had stopped the bus prior to it actually breaking the door, the large bulge protruding from the center clearly indicated what had happened. Dad was mortified. His co-bus drivers were quick to tell him that everything was fine but this was little consolation to Dad. While the bus itself was not damaged, the garage door would need to be replaced. While Dad was not financially responsible since the school's insurance policy covered the entire incident, he was certainly personally responsible. He never forgot this humbling experience and for years would endure the friendly bantering of his fellow bus drivers about his "safe driver" award during their morning coffee sessions. Good thing Dad had a good sense of humor and was able to laugh at his own mistakes.

This proved especially beneficial several months later when a new very young driver was hired to the bus driver's crew. The young man was a farmer who was much like Dad many years ago, in a situation where he was driving primarily to receive health care for his young family. He was obviously inexperienced and nervous just as Dad had been.

The routine for bus drivers at the end of the day was to caravan from the bus garage to the front of the school just in time to lineup for the kids to be dismissed from class. The buses, virtually less than a foot apart stretched the length of the entire front section of the school. Unfortunately the young driver who was positioned immediately behind Dad's bus cut the corner too sharp clipping the side mirror of Dad's bus. Dangling by an electric cord, Dad got off his bus and rushed to the bus of the young driver. The driver was mortified. Not only had he caused damage to the bus, he had managed to do this to the bus of the most seasoned and "decorated" veteran of the crew. Dad tried hard to keep a stern face as he entered the young man's bus, however immediately broke into laughter when he realized how upset the young driver was. Dad put his arm around the young lad and shared his accident story. They laughed hysterically as they realized how much they had in common. A bond that was formed that day that lasted for the rest of my father's life. Dad became a father figure for this man mentoring and collaborating on everything from farming to raising a family.

Settling into "Semi-retirement" Life

It was during this period of semi-retirement, time Dad became aware of the need for a first responder program in the small community of Westby. Dad had read about such programs in other communities and decided to share his idea with his friend Ron. Ron was community minded like Dad and between the two of them they gathered information and visited towns where such programs had been implemented. Without such a program the community, both people in the town as well people in the rural areas had to rely on an ambulance service and paramedic teams dispatched from a town seven miles away. Many times this meant delays and the lack of immediate assistance.

Mom wasn't too keen on the idea expressing her concern over liability and potential health risks. After all first responders were as the title says first on the scene and would most certainly be called upon to give mouth-to-mouth resuscitation and deal with body fluids. This was vintage Mom, on two accounts. First of all she was a private person. Being associated with this type of service put volunteers right in the middle of other people's lives. Secondly, she was by her own admission not a leader, instead being a willing follower and doer. She did not like the idea of Dad heading up such an initiative and was not shy to tell Dad how she felt.

Dad, while at least listening to Mom's concerns was known for carrying through on an idea if he felt it had merit. This was one of those cases where they finally decided to agree to disagree. Dad and Ron approached the City Council and County leaders about their idea and were pleased by the favorable response. With concept endorsements in hand, they went on about the job of trying to raise money to help fund the project and recruit potential volunteers. They would need some type of vehicle, preferably a van, some basic first-aid supplies, a dispatch radio system, volunteers and training.

To kick-off the fund raising efforts, they put on a pork feed with all the trimmings. Dad roasted a whole hog and about a dozen potential volunteers put together the rest of the meal. The event was successful on several counts. An elderly lady in town upon hearing of this initiative donated a used van which could be modified as a first responder vehicle. The money they generated from the hog roast was enough to provide the necessary modifications to the van, purchase supplies, and a new dispatch radio system. They were also pleased to find out that the training would be provided free of charge from the local hospital.

Within a couple of months from first talking about the concept of a First Responder program for Westby and the surrounding area they had formed a team of willing volunteers, modified van, and had all the supplies in place to get the program off the ground. A training schedule was in place and after several weeks of classes, including written as well as hands-on exams, they were ready to for their first emergency call; or at least they thought they were. It was late in the game when they realized the amount of paperwork required and what Dad would call "red tape" involved in establishing an official first responder program. Dad had underestimated this effort and was pleased to find that Ron was diligent in the paperwork process. He was tenacious, doing whatever it took to document and substantiate the program to government and healthcare officials and regulators. With approval of all the required documentation they officially became The Westby First Responders.

For Dad the training portion of becoming a First Responder was intense. It had been a while since he had actually spent any time "book-learning" which meant he had to spend more time than some reading and studying the material. Once the written exams were behind him however he was quick to grasp the necessary techniques first practicing on mannequins and eventually on real people.

Butterflies were in the stomachs of every responder when they finally received their first dispatch. It was lucky for those on call that day that the accident was a minor one. The injuries were non-life threatening and did not require any hospitalizations. As time passed however this would not be the case. They were a valuable resource to the people in the community of Westby, called upon to perform rescue and provide medical procedures that most of us would hope we would never have to experience. Being the first on the scene of an accident or medical emergency was a difficult assignment. This coupled with doing this job in a small community was truly a mixed blessing. The good part was that you knew most everyone that you were attempting to help. The bad news was that you knew most everyone that you were attempting help. It was difficult to maintain composure let alone your objectivity when you personally either knew the person you were helping or most certainly knew one of their immediate family members. This was especially the case when people suffered severe injuries or even worse death.

Throughout the years, Dad and the rest of the volunteer responders would grow and expand their efforts. They suffered minor setbacks such as when their donated van started on fire and was completely destroyed, however thanks to the generous donations from the community they were able to continue on. In fact as time passed donations were so generous they were able to purchase a state of the art emergency vehicle and equipment. Their training intensified as they were now required to meet additional state and federal certifications.

Dad viewed all of this as a positive experience. They were frequently asked to share their knowledge during school sponsored events and even put on a simulated drunk-driving crash prior to prom weekend. Dad was proud of his medical and first aid knowledge and was eager to share what he knew especially if he felt it might help to prevent accidents or injuries. He had an excellent rapport with the students many whom he had either driven to and from school each day or to and from school functions. He was a familiar face and someone they could trust.

After several very successful years in the basement waterproofing business, Dad decided it was time to sell the business. One of his bus kids who had worked for him during the summer months, now a grown adult, had shown interest in buying the business. Dad knew that he would do a good job and after a quick consultation with Mom they worked out a deal that was favorable to everyone.

Dad was now officially retired. At this point in time, he could have easily stopped driving bus however Dad would not hear of it. He continued driving his daily Bus Number 7 route in addition to driving for many extracurricular activities. He explained to people that driving bus gave Mom and him extra cash. The truth as anyone who really knew my father was that he was driving because he loved being around the young kids. His heavy involvement in school activities not only kept Mom and Dad very active in the community but kept them young at heart.

Living in town proved to really suit my Mom and Dad. They had always had a group of friends that they would play cards with on Sunday afternoons and occasionally go out for dinner and dancing with on Saturday evenings. But now they became very active in the church and other community events.

Almost every morning Mom would go for a walk with her friend Pat meeting up with several other friends at the local bakery for coffee and treats. Dad on the other hand would meet a group of his friends after driving bus at the local express (a diner located at the local gas station). They would shake dice and share stories. Mom referred to his group as the local gossip committee whereas her group of women she explained discussed worldly issues. This constant banter was very typical for Mom and Dad.

Mom also volunteered at the local second hand store and was active in her church circle. This meant she frequently served lunch and other meals at the church; mostly for funerals. As usual she never offered to lead any committees opting instead for being a "worker bee" as she would say.

In addition to Dad's bus and first responder activities, he was quick to help other people with projects. The next door neighbor for example, a young couple with small children, was having trouble with bats in the house. The father worked late afternoon/evening hours so Dad became the go-to person should a bat ever find its way into their house. One evening just as Mom and Dad were finishing dinner, the doorbell rang. There stood the youngest son of the next door neighbor screaming at the top of his lungs, "Richard, we have bats…come quick". Out the door Dad went with his tennis racket in tow. Dad quickly chased the bats out of the house and vowed to return the next day and repair a section in the roof where he suspected the bats had entered. It took several more trips, but finally the bat problem was taken care of. That little boy never forgot what my father did that evening and routinely called him the "bat defender".

Dad also enjoyed golf, fishing and woodworking. Golf was a sport that as a farmer he made a great deal of fun about. He thought how foolish it was for people to spend so much time chasing little white balls around. Once they moved into town however it was a different story. A former school bus rider took him golfing on several occasions providing him with lessons on the basics. With this bit of encouragement, he fell in love with the sport. He convinced Mom to try it and while reluctant at first, actually became proficient in her own right. They enjoyed many days of couples golf with friends followed by dinner at a restaurant.

They became members of the local Snowflake ski club course. Dad even co- purchased a golf cart with a buddy. Dad being his typical self, volunteered to make landscape improvements at the golf course. He spent many hours' meticulously planting and manicuring flowers and shrubs. The course looked beautiful with many accolades going to my father. Dad and his friends (some of which were ex school bus riders) played the course several days a week. Dad would organize games such as longest drive and other activities to add interest to the round. They would each contribute money into a "kitty" for distribution at the end of the round. To his golf buddies he was known as the organizer.

Much to his delight he actually had two holes in one during his time as a golfer. He was very proud of this accomplishment and was eager to tell the details of the shot to anyone who would listen.

While fishing had always been something Mom and Dad enjoyed, having more time now allowed them to meet their good friends Bob and Gloria for afternoon/evening adventures on the Mississippi River or area lakes. As was true to form most days ended with dinner at a nearby restaurant usually chatting with former school bus riders who recognized my father's bald spot on the back of his head.

Dad's interest in woodworking began in earnest when they moved to town. While he was always really handy with his hands building buildings and remodeling houses, he had never had the time to do anything very intricate. He decided to pursue woodcarving taking lessons and perfecting his craft to the point where he sold his work in stores and over the internet. He also became known for his ability to create furniture without a pattern. Word of mouth advertising from satisfied customers, many of which were his three generations of "school bus" clientele created a backlog of orders. He also created wooden horse rocking chairs donating them to an orphanage in Mexico. Even in retirement Dad continued to be an entrepreneur. He was a very creative; many would say quite an innovator.

Moving into town meant that my father could spend more time doing things he never had time for. One of those was taking care of the lawn. Their home was situated on a rather large lot with a sloped front yard. Dad strived to have the best manicured grass in the neighborhood. Bob, the neighbor across the street and Dad made a competition out of who could be the first to cut the grass in the spring. Dad usually won. He was also known to "hand paint" weeds and other unwanted foliage in his lawn with weed killer. One day one of his bus kids was playing across the street and observed my father sitting in the grass with an artist paintbrush. She ran to Dad's side and explained, "Richard, I didn't know that you were a painter". He chuckled and returned to his painting.

Another of Dad's hobbies was learning to play musical instruments. In particular he taught himself to play the harmonica and dulcimer. A dulcimer is a string instrument originally played in the Appalachian region of the United States. It is considered to be one of the easiest instruments to learn how to play, typically having only three to four strings played while laying it on your lap and then strumming or picking the strings to make music.

Dad would play for anyone who would listen including taking the harmonica on the bus route. The truth was, and Dad would admit this, he never mastered either of these instruments. For him it was all about the process, the fact that he was trying something new. He would be so tickled when he had learned a song and could share it with someone.

Life was good. They were enjoying retirement, hobbies and time with family and friends. This good fortune however was about to take a turn in another direction.

Illness Strikes my Dad

It was midafternoon on a Tuesday. I had been running errands. As I turned the corner to our street I noticed Mom and Dad's car in our driveway. Midafternoon on a Tuesday was an unusual day and time for Mom and Dad to stop by. As I pulled into the driveway, I noticed my husband and parents standing in the entrance way to the house. Somehow, I knew right away something was seriously wrong. As I entered the house, both Mom and Dad had tears in their eyes and proceeded to tell us that they had just come from the doctor's office where Dad had been diagnosed with cancer. Time seemed to stand still as we all went into the living room to better understand the situation. Mom and Dad had been on a chartered bus trip to the New York area with close friends Harold and Elaine when Dad discovered a lump on the side of his neck. The day before returning from the trip, he was shaving and happened to notice it as he was finishing the left side of his face. It was small, less than an inch in diameter but definitely something out of the ordinary.

The bus trip returned to La Crosse at approximately 11 am on that Tuesday morning. They had gone directly to the clinic to see if their general practice doctor could fit them into his schedule. Mom and Dad had both been patients of his for many years so when he heard they were in the waiting room and were eager to see him he made time. Upon visual examination he expressed concern that this in fact was not something to be taken lightly. He immediately performed a needle aspiration biopsy which involved removing a fluid sample from the lump via a needle. A simple lab test of the fluid concluded the existence of cancer. Within two days their lives had gone from no worries to now one of uncertainty. His doctor recommended Dad have a follow-up visit with a specialist to validate his findings and determine the proper course of action. That was it, nothing more to be done at this time. They left the clinic, drove the short drive to our house and shared the news.

We were all in a state of shock as we sat in the living room discussing the situation. Mom was very teary having trouble coming to terms with the diagnosis. Dad's mood, on the other hand quickly turned from sadness and disbelief to one of determination and strength. Within the hour he asked for a moment of silence and then loudly proclaimed that this "pity party" was over! No sense spending any more time dwelling on this he said, "how about we go get something to eat for dinner?" My husband, Joseph, knowing how much Dad liked his food, quickly offered to whip up dinner at the house. Dad was quick to accept this offer saying only if there would be leftovers for him to take home. His sense of humor had obviously returned. Mom decided to have a beer in her favorite tall glass. Joseph joined her. I had my usual glass of chardonnay and Dad his usual cranberry juice on the rocks.

We ended up sitting at the dining room table enjoying dinner and listening to stories from their trip. Mom sharing stories of the sites she had seen while Dad was most impressed by how the bus driver was able to maneuver the traffic and congestion in New York City. Certainly not the type of route you would want to put a "rookie" driver on was Dad's sentiment. The night ended with lots of hugs and plans to schedule the appointment with the specialist. Dad asked that we not share the news of his cancer until we knew more details. No need to worry anyone until we have more to go on Dad explained; and so it was.

Within the week we were gathered at the clinic for Dad's appointment with the specialist, an otolaryngologist, and (ear nose and throat doctor). He performed another needle aspiration biopsy. Unfortunately the outcome was the same. The tests confirmed the cancer diagnosis. This time they named the cancer. Dad had lymphoma. None of us knew much about this cancer however we were told that the next step was for us to see an oncologist. The oncologist would perform additional tests to confirm the specific type of lymphoma and determine the stage of the cancer.

Dad was eager to move forward with the next step choosing to see the first available oncologist verses waiting for one of the more senior staff. The first available was an Asian gentlemen by the name of Dr. Go. He was a young, small featured gentle man who immediately bonded with Dad.

During the first appointment he went out of his way to get to know Dad on a personal level. By the end of the first appointment he gave Dad's body the nickname "the bus". At the time Dad was approximately 220 pounds with a very large frame and barrel chest. Dr. Go knowing Dad's passion for school bus driving thought it only fitting that he call Dad's body this. This was the beginning of a long and very close relationship. Dad trusted Dr. Go impeccably. Dr. Go treated Dad with great respect.

The first round of tests included a bone marrow test. Dr. Go explained to Dad that there would be a delay as the technicians that administer the anesthesia for the bone marrow tests were already booked. The first available would be five days from now. Dad found this unacceptable telling Dr. Go that he would take the test without the anesthesia. It was at this point that Dr. Go began to understand and see the strong nature of Dad's will. Dr. Go explained that having a bone marrow test less anesthesia would be very painful thus advising against it. He explained that they basically bored a hole into your hip at which time they extract the marrow. Dad, however, would hear nothing of a delay and requested to move forward the next day with the test less anesthesia.

And so it was, the next day Dad took the bone marrow test plus a series of other tests. He did admit that the test was quite painful but short lived. Nothing that a little grit and determination couldn't pull you through were his words. He went on to explain that in his lifetime he had experienced worse pain. Not totally sure when that was however we decided to trust Dad on this one. By the end of that first week all the test results were back. We met late that week in Dr. Go's office to learn that Dad had stage four large cell diffused Non Hodgins lymphoma.

Mom and Dad met the news of the specific diagnosis with a great degree of optimism. Dad was absolutely convinced that he could beat whatever cancer came his way. He referred to Mom as his "rock" knowing she would stand firmly beside him throughout their journey. One of the ways Mom showed her conviction was by keeping Dad physically strong. She was determined to help keep his weight up during his treatments, even though at the time Dad could have afforded to lose some weight. Mom would hear nothing of it instead saying it was good that he had a cushion and that she would see to it that that cushion remained. She told Dr. Go that she intended to keep Dad's "bus" intact.

The news of Dad's cancer spread quickly. Dad shared the news with his bus family and within the day the rest of the community also knew. There was an immediate outpouring of cards, phone calls and well-wishers complete with casseroles and other treats. Dad assured everyone not to worry, that everything would be just fine. He greatly diminished the seriousness of the diagnosis promising his bus kids that he would not be needing to miss a day of driving. His supervisor at the bus garage reminded Dad that he had accumulated over 100 days of sick time so that time away was certainly not going to be an issue. Dad however saw it differently. He was going to do everything in his power to keep things normal for his bus kids.

Dad's Battle to Beat Cancer is On

One week after the diagnosis Dad started the strongest form of chemotherapy (RCHOP) available at the time. He had one treatment a month. Each treatment was very intense lasting a total of four hours. Fortunate for Dad, he had minimal side effects and came through the treatment with very little loss of weight. Dr. Go would tease him that he was still a bus. His only side effect was the loss of the rest of his hair. He had scheduled all his treatments around his bus schedule so for all practical purposes other than his bus kids teasing him about now being bald the effects of his cancer diagnosis were not visible.

Several months after Dad's chemotherapy treatments ended follow-up tests were performed to gauge the success of the chemo. Unfortunately the tests revealed that the cancer was still very active. Dad now had large tumors in his stomach in addition to smaller tumors throughout other areas of his body. Dad refused to accept any negative diagnosis instead requesting alternative treatments and therapies. He was determined to try everything available to beat the cancer.

The first option available to Dad was a new form of radiation. This treatment involved injecting a form of radiation directly into Dad's veins. It was a very risky, expensive and intense treatment. The day before the injection was to be administered, Dad was admitted to the hospital. He would undergo a series of tests to determine if he was eligible and capable of having the injection. Once the doctors determined he was eligible and capable, the radiation was "made" at the University of Minnesota hospital and driven by currier to the Gunderson Lutheran hospital in La Crosse. The nurse who brought the radiation into Dad's room was required to be in full hazardous material uniform. Not a spec of skin was present. The nurse was fully suited from head to toe. Once in place she pulled the radiation from the vile into a syringe and proceeded to inject it directly into Dad's blood stream. Dad would stay the night for observation only to repeat the process once a month for three months. Each injection was said to have cost in the range of $20K. Good thing Dad had good insurance.

Dad scheduled these appointments so as to only miss one evening bus route each month. He was determined to not let this cancer interfere with his bus driving. Secretly he told me he scheduled it this way so he wouldn't worry his bus kids. Scheduling in this manner was his way of telling them he was going to be ok.

Dad was once again fortunate as the side effects were very minimal. He had some nausea, flushing and a rash on his chest that both itched and burned. All in all he faired very well tolerating the injections with very little interference to their lifestyle.

Several months passed after the last radiation injection before follow-up tests could reveal what if any progress had been made in Dad's diagnosis. Unfortunately once again the news was not favorable. Dr. Go regrettably informed Dad that the cancer remained with several of the tumors growing in size and intensity.

The next form of treatment that Dad decided to pursue was aggressive radiation treatments. The radiologist was a very abrasive, cocky, and persuasive person. During the initial visit Mom and I were not impressed by his style however Dad found his confidence and experience compelling. The doctor told us that he was like a skilled welder. He would be able to eliminate the cancer by skillfully targeting the tumors with high dose radiation. He was sure that he could give Dad several good months or years of no cancer. Dad agreed to the treatment plan enduring 45 days of radiation to the stomach area. During this time he suffered serious stomach problems including many bouts with diarrhea. Mom worked diligently to make sure Dad did not lose too much weight. She was pleased when the treatment ended and he had only lost 20 pounds. We were all delighted when at the one month follow-up appointment we learned that the tumors in the stomach had shrunk by over half. His arrogant doctor was quick to remind us that this was just as he had promised!

Again during this entire 45 day timeframe Dad never missed a day of bus driving. He scheduled his radiation in the middle of the day allowing him to drive both his morning and evening route. As far as his bus kids knew, other than losing a little bit of weight Richard was doing just fine.

Three months later during a routine follow-up visit with Dr. Go, he performed a routine exam on Dad only to reveal that the tumors in his stomach area had returned. In fact, Dr. Go for the first time could feel the tumors during the physical exam. Dr. Go told Dad that his "bus" was once again in trouble. At this point, all treatments within the Gunderson Clinic domain had been exhausted. The only options left available were experimental treatments otherwise known as clinical trials.

Dr. Go explained the challenges with clinical trials. These challenges fell into two buckets. First, was the patient's ability to qualify for the treatment. The protocol for many of the experimental treatments was very strict and depending upon the stage the clinical trial was in the number of participants could be very limited. A person needed to be thoroughly examined and tested in order to make sure that they met all the conditions of the treatment.

The second challenge dealt with the side effects of the clinical trial. Many times experimental treatments had serious if not potential life threatening side effects. The patient needed to be fully informed and consent to knowing and understanding the risks before being allowed into the program.

Par for the course, Dad was not willing to give up. He dismissed any challenges related to the clinical trials and the experimental nature of the treatments. He pressed Dr. Go for details on how best to move forward. Dad was eager to get moving. Knowing there was going to be no stopping him, Dr. Go immediately made the referral and connections to the Mayo Clinic in Rochester. Dad was pleased. Next stop he proclaimed was to the Mayo Clinic in Rochester, Minnesota for potential inclusion in experimental programs. He told everyone that asked about his progress this was his next best option. He was sure there was "something" out there that would cure his cancer.

Our first visit to Mayo clinic occurred in May. Dad was eager to get through the screening process and begin treatment. He was excited that if timed right he would have the treatment during the summer thus avoiding any downtime from bus driving and time away from his kids. The first visit was overwhelming. It was such a large facility. Multiple tests were required, each test in a different building and with a different doctor. During this time Mom and I took on a very critical, almost consultant role critiquing every part of the Mayo experience. We wanted to be sure that Dad was treated properly and that he was not put into a situation that was too risky.

Dad's primary doctor at Mayo, who was working with us to summarize his tests and determine viability for admittance into an experimental program happened to be a very arrogant person. He asked us numerous technical questions about Dad's diagnosis and previous treatments in what felt like to Mom and me in a condescending manner as if he were trying to intimidate or humble us. Mom and I did not care for this doctor, however Dad thought he was ok. After all Dad said, "we can overlook a little arrogance if this guy can help me get into a program that cures my cancer". Guess you can't argue with that. This was par for the course. Dad was a very excepting person quick to overlook any unusual personality quirks.

Dad passed the preliminary tests so next up were two bone marrow tests. Once again medicated tests would have delayed progress by roughly two weeks so Dad chose to undergo two non-medicated bone marrow tests. These tests proved to be the last non medicated tests Dad would take. Subsequent to the tests, he decided two in one day was too much! Any future bone marrow tests would need anesthesia.

Unfortunately as they prepped him for the second bone marrow the attending physician noticed a lump near his groin area. Sure enough another tumor had surfaced. He was immediately taken to St. Mary's hospital in Rochester where a biopsy was performed. As suspected, it was cancerous.

Despite this, Dad was admitted into the experimental program. Dad, as you can imagine, was super excited to be a part of this experimental program. The doctor reviewed details about the program complete with possible complications and side effects. He was going to be a part of a clinical trial that was in phase one. Phase 1 of a clinical trial means it is the first time that a new drug or treatment procedure is tested on humans. The purpose of this phase of medical research is to determine the safety of the test procedure and also demonstrate that the results found in the pre-clinical trials (studies done on cell cultures and animals, for example) can be duplicated in humans. Phase 1 trials have a higher amount of risk due to the fact that not much is known about the effects of the drug on humans. He went on to say that for this trial very few participants, typically in the area of 50 were included. Dad beamed proud to be a part of this select group to test this new drug and procedure. The doctor also told him how lucky he was to have been chosen as the inclusion/exclusion criteria for this particular trial was very strict with preference given to only the healthiest volunteers. The doctors were impressed by how physically strong Dad was despite the various treatments he had endured and were especially impressed by his positive attitude. Mom of course proudly took credit for Dad's physical strength telling doctors of her mission was to keep Dad strong. The doctors smiled patting both Mom and Dad on the shoulder welcoming them into this elite group.

In March of that year, 2006, Dad found out that he had been nominated for "the Teacher of the Year" award. Two of his passengers, both in their senior year at Westby, learned of the program run by the local TV station to recognize top-notch teachers throughout the Coulee Region and decided to nominate Dad for this award. While they acknowledged that Dad did not "technically" meet the true definition of teacher they felt strongly that Dad had taught them more than many of their classroom teachers and thus pursued his nomination.

Although Dad did not "win" he took great pride and satisfaction in the role he had played in the lives of his riders and also enjoyed the recognition both in the local newspaper as well as on TV as the local La Crosse station which sponsored the award conducted an interview with Dad and aired his interview several times.

The following is the article (written by Dorothy Jasperson) that the Westby Times published about Dad and his nomination for teacher of the year.

Ekern rolls through life not sweating the little things.

Richard Ekern, of Westby, has traveled many miles and he's still rolling with the punches and influencing the lives of students he's hauled from their homes to school for 51 one of his 73 years living in Vernon County.

Growing up on a farm with three brothers and two sisters, Ekern, learned early on that anything worth having is worth fighting for and sweating the little things just demands more deodorant. When life gets him down he heads to his workshop in the garage and spends hours carving beautiful creations out of walnut, cherry, oak or whatever piece of nature's element he has at his disposal.

"When I'm carving time just fades away along with any the stress of the day. Before I know it my life is back on track," Ekern said.

Ekern's life has been slightly off track since 2004 when he noticed a lump in his neck and learned from doctors he had developed Non-Hodgkin's Lymphoma. The lump he discovered was one of many which had been manifesting themselves throughout his body unbeknown to him. He did what he had to do to counteract the problem by placing his faith in the medical staff at Gundersen Lutheran's Cancer Center and more importantly in his optimistic attitude toward life. After all, he felt fine and he wasn't about to let cancer rock his world.

He started an intensive series of chemotherapy treatments to fight the cancer which had invaded his body. Unlike the majority of chemotherapy patients who have adverse side effects to the strong chemotherapy drugs, Ekern was one of the fortunate few who never suffered from the nausea, vomiting and days of total fatigue after treatments. He lost his hair and was weak at times, but felt blessed to have avoided the rest of the side effects associated with chemotherapy treatment.

Throughout the entire chemotherapy treatment process Ekern remained true to his dedication to driving school bus in the Westby Area School District. He only missed a few afternoon routes when his treatments were running behind. After 51 years of driving he's become a friend to hundreds of kids and a familiar face to families on Lovaas Ridge and down the winding roads of Spring Coulee. He's silently watched as children he greeted with a friendly smile twice a day as they stepped on bus #7 grew into adults, married and began raising their own families.

The Clifford Bakkum family of rural Westby can attest to that. Early on in his career Ekern greeted Clifford in the morning and afternoon as he rode the bus to school. When Clifford married Mary after graduation, their son, Brian became the second generation of Bakkums to ride on Ekern's bus. Today Brian and his wife Jodi's children, Danielle, Jacob, Megan and Nicole are Ekern's third generation of Bakkums to step on board the Ekern express. For Ekern it's like being a part of many families. He's learned to read the emotions of children who are happy, sad or struggling through difficult times growing up. He's felt the pain for families who've lost loved ones and tried silently to help when others were in need.

Ekern has influenced many lives without words. He's done so by safely getting them home and controlling behavior problems on board his bus from the driver's seat. He's provided a friendly face when children needed it the most. He's read stories, poems and observed the artistic talents of kids who proudly hand him their creations for review when they hop on board the school bus.

"It's so much fun to try and guess what kids draw and watch their faces when you guess wrong. They call you silly and laugh at you out loud. The innocence of kids is so refreshing because they're not afraid to tell you what they think, they don't hold grudges and they respect your opinion," Ekern said.

Ekern's devotion and love of his job paid off recently when two students on his bus decided to recognize him for his ability to teach students from the front of the bus, not from the front of the classroom.

Krista Ike and Loni Olstad, both seniors at Westby Area High School, have been passengers on Ekern's bus since kindergarten. They knew about a program through WKBT Channel 8 in La Crosse which recognizes top-notch teachers throughout the Coulee Region and rewards them with a segment on the evening news and the use of a donated vehicle to drive at their leisure for one month. Ike and Olstad believe education isn't just an acquired skill in the classroom, but one that's nurtured from the time a student leaves home. So they set a plan in action to honor Ekern, a man they both have the utmost respect for.

Ike compiled a letter to Channel 8 asking them to consider taking education out of the classroom and honoring Ekern for his unlimited patience, kindness, respect and ability to teach children without a chalkboard or pencils and paper. She nominated him for the top-notch teacher program. Her attempt at top-notch teacher was declined, but Ekern was awarded his moment of fame and was featured last week on the evening news. He didn't get the use of a vehicle for a month, but for him the nomination by Ike and Olstad was worth more than a fleet of cars.

"We've both rode Richard's bus since we were kids. He always greets us with a smile which starts the day off right. If we've had a bad day it doesn't matter when we get on the bus in the afternoon, because we know that same smile will make the day better on the ride home," Krista said.

Olstad added, "A lot of kids wouldn't dream of still riding the bus as seniors in high school, but Richard makes the ride a pleasant experience. He has a way with kids and it's an honor to have been along for the ride."

Tears welted up in Ekern's eyes when he listened to the girls speak so kindly about him. A humble man, with a heart of gold, Ekern and his wife, Ilene, celebrated their 54th wedding anniversary on Feb. 23, the same day he was preparing to take part in a clinical medical trial with the new cancer fighting drug Sorafenib.

Ekern learned on Feb. 7 that the tumors he'd been battling to shrink for two years were growing again. The initial chemotherapy had destroyed the majority of the problem, but larger tumors behind his heart and in his stomach had resisted the chemo and any additional medical treatments he received after it ended. Ekern will be one of only 41 people throughout the United States participating in the clinical trial. He's been through a series of examinations, blood tests, scans, EKGs and had more than his share of bone marrow biopsies.

"My physician believes I'm an ideal candidate for this clinical trial. If I can help anyone in the future from contracting this disease, it's worth the chances I'll take participating in a trial study. I trust God, my *doctor and I'm keeping a positive attitude about the entire thing," Ekern said.*

For Ekern nothing ventured is nothing gained. If he doesn't try to combat the recently manifested cancer it'll control his life. The only person Ekern wants controlling his life is himself, or maybe his wife, who he refers to as the "rock" which has brought him this far and helps keep him in the game. His children, Reid, Renee, Randall and Todd have been there every step of the way along with overwhelming community support.

Ekern doesn't have time to dwell on things he can't change. He prefers facing things head on and finding the silver lining in any situation. He racked up a hole in one in 2005, a feat even some of the world's best golfers haven't accomplished. He's got plenty of golfing in his plans and trips to the river to hook a few big ones. His woodcarving orders are growing and before long the grass will be green and the lawn will need mowing. For now he's enjoying life, looking forward to the future and keeping one eye in the rear view mirror on bus #7.

Dad completed all the necessary paperwork for the clinical trial and within a week received the "pills" that would let him partake in the experimental program. As with most experimental programs the patient does not know if they are a part of the active drug or if they are receiving a placebo. Dad was absolutely convinced that he was receiving the active drug. By now everyone in their community was aware of the news. Richard had qualified for a clinical trial and was one of a handful of people across the world that would be receiving this drug. It was almost as though he had achieved celebrity status.

Dad was just four doses into the program when he developed intense abdominal pain. This was at an intensity Dad had never encountered before. He was barely able to get out of bed and into the car for Mom drive him to the emergency room. She took him directly to the La Crosse hospital, roughly 45 minutes from their home only to have the doctors dismiss the symptoms as related to "something Dad must of ate." She explained that Dad had just started a clinical trial as part of the Mayo Clinic however the Doctors expressed no interest in exploring anything further instead giving him a mild sedative and sending him home

The next night the same thing occurred with the same outcome. By the third night Dad woke to uncontrollable stomach spasms and vomiting. By now Mom was at her wits end. She called the First Responders. Mom heard the dispatch come across the CB in their kitchen and was relieved to know that Dad's team would soon be there to help. Within a few minutes they arrived at the house. One of the women on call that evening had been one of Dad's bus kids. She assured Mom that when they got Dad to the hospital she would personally make sure Doctors would take Dad's symptoms seriously this time. The team skillfully laid Dad on the gurney and maneuvered the steep staircase of their one hundred year old home. Within ten minutes Dad was in the ambulance and on his way to the hospital.

This time he was admitted to the hospital. The pain in his abdomen was very intense. My Dad who rarely complained about anything was beside himself. Numerous tests were done without any conclusive results. Finally as a last resort the doctors decided to do exploratory surgery. The doctor's called this a discovery surgery however nothing major was discovered. They removed his gall bladder as a possible solution however in the end concluded that it really had nothing to do with the real problem.

Days later Dad continued to have problems. He had now been in the hospital for five days. The pain continued. At this point he was in and out of consciousness and at times was delirious. They ordered additional tests including a colonoscopy none of which provided any diagnosis or relief. The entire family including grandkids had assembled at the hospital. We were taking turns staying the night providing Mom an opportunity to take a break from the hospital. There were also several nurses on staff who were ex bus kids that provided additional support and care when times really got tough. One evening during a time when Dad was actually quite comfortable he started talking about what he would do with a million bucks. He told us he would donate the money to the Westby auditorium.

He wanted to make sure that all his talented bus kids had a place where they could practice and perform at their highest level. He was sure that the planning committee could put the money to good use. We all chuckled knowing that Dad's heart would always be with his community and especially with his bus kids!

By now, a large team of doctors at Gunderson were assigned to Dad's case. Dr. Udell and Dr. Go consulted with Mayo to understand if Dad could have reacted so negatively to the clinical trial after only four doses. The doctors overseeing the clinical trial doubted the experimental drug could be the cause of his problem. One of the doctors on Dad's case labeled him the "mystery man." We were assured by one of the hospital administrators (an ex bus kid) that the best minds at Gunderson/Lutheran were working his case.

Despite all this focus, Dad's condition continued to worsen. His blood counts continued to fluctuate dropping to very low levels. His liver and pancreas were inflamed. The outlook was grave. Late one evening while I was staying with Dad he developed a very high fever and heart irregularities. He was immediately moved to the cardiac intensive care floor. Despite the late hour the Doctors encouraged us to notify family members. They were not sure if Dad would make it through the night. While I was waiting for the others to arrive I was sitting with Dad and noticed a rash on his face and chest. The doctors performed a biopsy and within an hour were able to make the diagnosis of a rare strain of chicken pox. In the end Doctors concluded that Dad's suppressed immune system as a result of the clinical trial had allowed his body to deteriorate and the infection to manifest.

He was moved to an isolation room within the cardiac intensive care unit and given strong anti-viral/antibiotic drugs intravenously. He was monitored very closely to see if his body was going to be able to kick in and fight off this infection. Doctors gave him less than a 50% chance. The days came and went without any noticeable improvement. Finally after almost a week he began to show signs of recovery. While slow at first within four days he was back to his normal self with the exception of lot of "pox" and a slightly smaller "bus". He had lost 30 pounds during this time. Mom was eager to get him home to nurse him back to his pre illness weight. She even started sneaking in special treats to the hospital in an effort to begin the process. After three weeks in the hospital he was told he could leave the hospital but would need to go to a nursing home to recover. He would need to regain mobility and strength before he could go home. Dad disagreed with this course of action insisting he was well enough and strong enough to bypass the nursing home. He failed to realize the toll three weeks in bed had taken on his body. It became very apparent however the first time he tried to get out of bed on his own. "Nursing home sounds like a good plan", he exclaimed as he struggled to gain his balance and walk the 30 steps required for a hospital discharge. The next day the paperwork was complete and his discharge was granted.

Dad's nursing home experience was not the best, as he would describe it. He was admitted to Vernon Manor in Viroqua. Mom and Dad had visited many times and thought it was well suited for Dad's needs. He also knew quite a few of the staff many of which were in one way or another related to his bus kids. He would be in good company and well taken care of. The challenge was Dad was not satisfied. The confined space of his tiny room and small bed coupled with the bland food and lack of activities he enjoyed left him not very happy. We were able to rectify most of the challenges by putting a large mattress in the room, having Mom bring in his favorite foods and his golf clubs. The facility had a large grassy area complete with gazebo area. Once Dad felt better, he could practice his golf swing. The real problem however was he was bored. He desperately wanted to get home and resume his normal activities. Summer was now in full swing. He was eager to recover and resume bus driving in the fall.

One day I suggested to Dad that it would be good for him to reflect on his many years as a bus driver. I offered to take notes and transcribe his words. He thought about it for a while and then with a big grin on his face said he thought this would be super. Thanks Toots, the name he called me since childhood, I believe this is just what I need right now! We started the very next day and continued for roughly a week. Each time I would sit with him he would recount what he affectionately referred to as the many seasons of driving. He loved to tell stories and share his memories. By the second day several of the staff would gather to listen to him. He loved the interaction. His health improved significantly during this time. Not only did his appetite return but the spark in his eyes, the pace of his walk and his overall attitude improved. By the end of the second week Dad was swinging a golf club and engaging in planned activities. He was ready to be released. My notes from those conversations are included below.

Seasons of Driving

During my father's many years of driving school bus he experienced a variety of seasons; the four seasons that were a part of the Wisconsin climate; the seasons associated with the school year and the seasons or changes that occurred in the family structure during his fifty three years of driving.

The climate in Wisconsin's includes spring, summer, autumn and winter seasons; with the largest portion of the calendar year spent in the winter season.

As a bus driver you are presented with every season; from warm, balmy, humid 90 degree days when the un-air conditioned bus becomes basically a sweat box full of overheated rowdy kids opening and closing windows at whim to sub-zero temperatures, heavy snowfall winters when the bus takes on the feel of the frozen tundra. The heating system within the bus is unable to warm the drafty confines. The plastic seats remain stiff and inflexible throughout the duration of the route. Spring is a combination of the winter snow fall melting and frequent rain showers; both of which can cause challenges for the bus, the driver and its passengers. Autumn is the calmest time of year with the route relatively easy to maneuver while providing many picturesque landscapes of fall colors.

The rural areas surrounding Westby, a small historically primarily Norwegian community, include a combination of hills, or ridgetops, and valleys with drops in altitude of greater than five hundred feet. This type of landscape coupled with the climate in the region adds a certain level of complexity to driving a school bus. Dad's route happened to include some of the most extreme terrain in the area. The combination of extreme variation in landscape and weather conditions led to some interesting experiences. Whether it was thunderstorms, washed out roads caused by driving rain, hail, or blizzards, Dad drove through them all.

One of Dad's biggest frustrations was when the school administrator would decide to close school due to bad weather. While Dad could certainly understand the concern of the administration, he also felt that the school administration underestimated the skill of their bus drivers. After all my Dad would say, "We are professional drivers. No need to call off school due to a little bad weather." Guess that was a little of my Dad's strong-willed Norwegian mother Martha's attitude showing.

Despite Dad's confidence in his driving skills, he did encounter some interesting experiences related to weather while driving his route. On one occasion he was driving his bus down a steep road that connected the ridgetop to the valley when suddenly his bus hit a patch of black ice. It was early spring and the snow had just started to melt. The bright sun of the day had melted the snow creating a small pond covering most of the road. Just as Dad's bus came lumbering around the last corner he realized that this particular section of the road was shielded from the sun. The shady area made the road conditions hard to predict and while he first thought the road was just wet, he soon realized that this was not the case. What had once been water was now ice.

Before Dad could even apply his brakes the back of the bus slid off the road and out over an embankment. Luckily he was able to control the front end and stop the engine before it slid any further. There he was stranded, half on the road, half off. It was as though the bus was a teeter-totter pivoting forward and backward on the shoulder of the road. The back tires and rear of the bus hanging free high above the forty foot drop to the ravine below. The front tires, firmly planted, gripping for all their might onto the gravel road. Dad took a big breath, said a silent prayer and immediately turned his attention to the kids that were on board.

The kids were screaming at the top of their lungs each projecting at a different decibel level. He knew that the bus was in a precarious position. Any sudden shift in any sizable amount of weight could easily send the bus off the embankment. His six foot one inch two hundred and twenty pound body needed to stay firmly planted in the driver's seat. He glanced in his rear view mirror as tried as best he could to project his voice in a calm yet commanding manner. Seeing that this was not helping to calm the kids, he carefully pivoted his seat and turned around to face the kids. There were a total of twelve kids on board. He knew that there was no way for him to get the bus back on the road so he knew he his first priority was to get the kids safely off the bus. Trying to connect with them by looking into each of their eyes he proceeded to tell them to stay in their seats and to stop screaming. He reassured them that everything was going to be just fine. He explained that the trick in this situation was to be as calm and as quiet as they could be. Quiet as mice and calm as a sleeping baby he went on to explain. He later admitted that this was the farthest thing from his mind but knew that any sudden commotion could cause tragic consequences. Then, starting with the child in the seat furthest back in the bus he talked to each one by name, instructing them to very slowly get up and walk to the front of the bus. He gathered them all next to him as he gave instructions on what they were to do next. He said he was going to open the door and each one of them was to step carefully off the bus and then run as fast as they could up a small hill to a clearing approximately twenty feet away. There they were to wait for further instructions. He gingerly opened the bus door and the kids did just as they had been instructed. The older kids helped the younger ones and within a matter of minutes Dad was the only one left on the bus.

The only method of communication on buses during this time was a CB radio. He reached for the speaker and radioed the bus garage to tell his boss, the head mechanic of his predicament. Dad was relieved to hear his boss answer as quickly as he did and was even more relieved to hear how calm and reassuring the sound of his boss's voice was. Within twenty minutes from making the call, Dad saw a police car and large tow truck come around the corner. His boss was riding with the driver of the tow truck and immediately ran to check on Dad who was still firmly planted in the driver seat. It wasn't until the tow truck had secured two wenches to the front of the bus that Dad was told he could come off the bus. The police officer was tending to the kids giving them words of praise for their brave actions. Once off the bus, Dad ran to where the kids were gathered and together they watched the large tow truck moan and groan as it struggled to pull the bus back onto the road. They all cheered and hugged as their Bus Number 7 was rescued and parked safely on the side of the gravel road. As quickly as the drama had unfolded, it was now behind them.

A careful inspection of the bus revealed that there was no damage to the bus. Luckily everyone was safe and uninjured. Other than frayed nerves they were all going to be just fine. Within an hour after the incident they were all back on the bus. Although still shaking inside over what had just happened, Dad did his best to exhibit outward confidence as he once again took his place behind the wheel and took command of the bus. He told the twelve kids that he knew they were probably a bit scared to get back on the bus but assured them that if they faced their fears together they would be able to move forward. He finished his morning run and delivered the kids to school two hours late. The kids were delighted with the late arrival, with a truly valid reason to be late, and bustled with chatter as they left the bus. The original twelve kids were already retelling and elaborating on the morning's excitement. They had a great story to tell and couldn't wait to share the details with their classmates, teachers and family members. Dad received numerous calls and cards of thanks from the parents of not only the twelve kids that had been stranded on the bus but from other families on his route as well. They were grateful for his quick actions and calm spirit. Needless to say a special bond was formed between the twelve young riders, their families and Dad.

On yet another occasion, this time a rather humorous event Dad was taking a fully loaded bus of kids home from school when snowy conditions turned into a full blown white-out. A white-out is a term used when blowing and falling snow becomes so dense that you can no longer see in front of you. It is much like what happens when fog creates zero visibility. The driving winds in the valley where Dad's route was created two to three foot snow drifts across various sections of the road and now the wind was tossing the snow around in every direction. The bus bucked as Dad simultaneously downshifted and accelerated with just the right amount of intensity to avoid getting the bus stuck in the snow drift. Dad welcomed these conditions and relished the chance to show off his driving skills. It was almost as though he was challenging the weather conditions to give him yet another obstacle when the wind shifted and he was faced with white-out conditions. He was driving blind. He steadied the wheel and gently tapped the brakes preparing to stop the bus just as the wind died down and visibility returned. As he stared out the windshield he realized that they had veered off the road. The bus had gone over a large drift, passed down a small hill through a shallow ditch and was now traveling on a plowed corn field.

Dad immediately stopped the bus and jumped out to assess the situation. Everything was fine. The kids were all fine and in fact most of them had no idea what had just happened. The bus was fine. The ditch had been very shallow and the field flat and relatively smooth. As Dad considered his options he couldn't help but notice that the plowed field had very little snow covering it. The direction of the wind combined with the location of the field relative to the road had blown most of the loose snow from the field to the road. As only my Dad could tell it, he had three options.

One, he could turn the bus around and try to retrace their steps driving the bus back up the incline, through the ditch, over the large drift and down the snowy road. As he stared at the cookie trail left by the bus, he concluded this would be too risky. He no longer had the speed and momentum of a moving bus and knew this was needed to maneuver the uphill obstacles. Odds were high that they would get stuck, need to call for a tow and worst of all would be stranded on the bus for who knows how long. Declining conditions meant that a speedy response from the tow truck and/or replacement bus would slow at best. All in all, Dad concluded that this option was not desirable.

His second option would be to just call his boss at the bus garage, tell him what had happened, give him their coordinates and wait for the tow truck and/or replacement bus. Although less risky, he again came back to the fact that with declining weather conditions the wait would be unpredictable and most likely long. Again, he decided this option was not desirable.

Finally, his third option would be to simply drive down the corn field until he reached a spot where he felt he could go through the ditch and back onto the road. Dad liked this idea; in fact he liked the idea a lot. It avoided any need for a tow and would get the kids home safely and in a timely manner.

He told the kids what he was going to do and was pleased to find they totally supported his idea. He prepared them for the trip telling them to sit up straight and to hold on to the back of the seat in front of them. Once everyone was securely in their seats, he fastened his seat belt and started the engine. He shifted into low gear and hit the accelerator. Slowly at first then beginning to gain speed, the bus lumbered down the plowed corn field. The kids were pretending to ride a bucking bronco as they shouted "hey ah" and "giddy up". Dad was oblivious, concentrating on locating a place where he could safely maneuver the bus from the field to the road. Finally he noticed a place where the ditch was shallow and the drifts were minimal. With a quick acceleration he skillfully made the transition. Once back on the road the kids chanted" hip-hip-hooray" followed by a rousing chorus of "for he's a jolly good fellow". What a wild ride. Dad was relieved as the last kid was delivered safely home and he started to reflect on the events of the day.

The kids were quick to tell their parents about their exciting ride. Dad thought he might receive some negative feedback about his decision but was instead pleased to receive calls from parents thanking him for getting their kids home safely before the weather got even worse. Conditions got so bad in fact that school was closed for three days as the snow, wind and freezing temperatures gripped the area. When school finally resumed Dad learned that his rather unorthodox method had earned him the title of "renegade man" among his bus families and fellow bus drivers. The term stuck with Dad for years to come.

The change of seasons in this area of the country meant more than extreme weather conditions. It also meant the growth of plants, flowers, vegetables and fruits that were only available for a short time each year. Through the years, Dad bus route had become his very own treasure trove for many of these items. He knew exactly when and exactly where to find the valued items and looked forward to being the first driver to return to the bus garage with the latest flower or produce in hand.

His absolute favorite time of year however was early spring. You see my mother loved pussy willows. For those of you that are not familiar, they are long brown willow sticks with white/grey puffs scattered throughout. They grow in swampy-marshy areas and can be found for only a short time every spring. Many of the coulees on Dad's route included swampy areas which were conducive to the growth of pussy willows. Every spring like clockwork Dad would be on the lookout for pussy willows, carefully watching them grow until they reached just the right level of maturity. Then during one of his afternoon runs, he would stop the bus and proceed to cut Mom a large bouquet. Dad's bus kids knew the ritual and eagerly joined in the search cheering loudly when Dad would return with his prized possession. She would be thrilled when Dad would surprise her with a fresh cut arrangement upon returning from his route.

Mom's other favorite was fresh lilacs. Dad was known to stop his bus, mid route, complete with a load of kids on board, in order to cut fresh lilacs. He knew that in order to ensure the most fragrant and beautiful bouquet, he had to cut the lilacs at just the right time. The kids knew that no matter how much they would heckle or tease Dad about doing this nothing was going to stop him from getting the flowers for Mom. It had become a ritual for the kids of Bus Number 7.

During the fall season, Dad's bus route families would encourage him to help himself to their gardens. By this time of the year their gardens were overflowing with tomatoes, cucumbers, and squash and assorted other goodies. He could hardly contain himself routinely showing off his good fortune to his co-drivers at the bus garage before bringing his stash home to Mom.

While the seasons of the year certainly presented their share of challenges for Dad and his bus route, his biggest challenges came in the seasons of change he experienced relative to the family structure. When Dad first started to drive bus, in the mid 1950's all of the mothers on Dad's route were stay-at-home-moms with husbands who farmed and worked the land. The family unit was strong with a focus on hard work and solid values. Meals were prepared from scratch and families ate together. Welfare even if available was unheard of. Generations of families and neighbors would work together in time of need providing for any among them that may have a need.

In the case of Dad's route, most of the farms had been handed down from generation to generation. Neighbors had known each other for years and it was extremely uncommon for people to ever leave. There was a strong Norwegian presence which could be not only heard in the accents of many of the people but also by their customs and mannerisms. For the most part no frills, stoic people. They saw to it that their children had breakfast and well clothed before sending them on their way to school. Rarely was there not at least one parent waving at the door, both when he picked them up in the morning and when he dropped them off in the late afternoon.

As time passed divorce was more prevalent, more single-parent households. Regardless of marital status many mothers now worked outside of the home. This meant a child might be by themselves to catch the bus in the morning or be dropped off at the end of the day to an empty house. Dad would do his best to understand each child's situation so as to better handle any special needs or circumstances.

As the years went on, and times continued to change, he encountered families who were experiencing difficulties ranging from alcoholism to drug abuse to extreme poverty. For my father, he viewed this as an opportunity to heighten and expand his role in the lives of his kids doing whatever he could to boost a child's self-esteem and build confidence. He viewed himself as having the ability to make a difference in his kids' lives.

He stocked his bus with snacks, clothes and basic school supplies just in case he discovered one of his kids needed something. During the winter months he carried a supply of extra hats, mittens, and scarves for those emergency days when someone might forget these on the way out the door. He was even known to purchase a winter coat when he noticed one of his kids was not dressed for the harsh winter conditions. He handled these situations with great care so as to not embarrass the child or parents. His relationship was so strong with both his kids and parents this was never an issue.

Then came the era when bus drivers were trained on child abuse. My father and other drivers were now required to report any noticeable day-to-day changes both physical and mentally in their kids. They were also trained and were required to report changes to family dynamics or physical changes in the home. They were in a unique position to assess both the child and their physical external home environment.

Unfortunately, on a couple of occasions Dad had to file a report. This was extremely distressing for my father. It was beyond his comprehension to think that a child would be abused or be living in an unsafe or unstable environment. As such, he became each child's biggest advocate going to extreme measures to intervene as needed.

One of the more difficult things for Dad was when the school district announced new rules relative to physical boundaries. No longer were teachers, bus drivers or anyone associated with the school district allowed to touch a student. The rules were first instituted to the school teachers but later made their way to the bus drivers

Dad was very upset by this change; "what was the world coming to", he would explain to anyone that would listen to him. You see Dad was known for his hugs, pats on the back and words of encouragement. His kids had grown accustomed to his affection and were equally as upset with the new policy. Dad did his best to comply with the rules, however one of his more ingenious kids circulated a document allowing the kids and their parents to sign a waiver allowing Dad to continue with his affection.

The seasons of the school year brought different moods to the job of driving bus. The beginning of the school year meant excitement for most, new clothes, new backpacks and supplies and in many cases nervous first riders. The youngest of dad's riders held a special place in his heart. He took great care to do what he had to make them comfortable having preschoolers sit directly behind him.

Also for kids moving into the district and riding bus for the first time he took care to know their names and greet them accordingly. He also would pair them up with a seasoned veteran to make sure that at least for the first couple of months they had a riding companion. Dad believed this accomplished two things. First it gave the new kid someone to pass the time with and for those he asked to be a "buddy", provided them an opportunity to be a leader and set a positive example for others.

The Christmas season meant lots of holiday cheer. The weeks just before the holidays would be filled with homemade cards and goodies. Dad loved this time of year, relishing in all the attention and delicious treats. The week of Christmas, Dad would treat his kids with soda and chips. He always purchased more than needed to make sure that everyone received the flavor of their choice. If one of the kids on his route, had a sibling that was not yet of age to ride the bus, he would send along extras for them.

The long season of winter meant tougher than normal road conditions and many times school delays or cancellations. In addition kids were picked up when it was still dark out and returned home in darkness. This presented several challenges to a rural bus driver. Not only did he have to navigate the treacherous rural roads and narrow driveways, he was most concerned about who would be home for the child if school happened to cancel or end early. To help alleviate his concern, he had the parents fill out details about where their kids should be dropped off in case of an emergency.

The spring was met with excitement as the school year ended and more sunlight in the day. Kids were eager to be done with the routine of the school year and routinely exhibited more playful sometimes rowdy behavior. Much like Dad's holiday tradition, soda and chip treats were again shared however rather than provide this treat at the end of the school day, he gave the kids this treat on the way to school. Dad had a mischievous streak. By now he knew many of the teacher quite well and knew that giving caffeine and treats in the morning he would make their school day a little more challenging. Routinely teachers would stop by his bus while in the lineup for the end of the day run and "thank" Dad for his generosity.

It also was a rather bittersweet time of year for the kids that were graduating. Dad had been with them from preschool thru twelve years of education. He watched them grow and develop both physical and mentally. Many tears were shed during the final ride. Mom and Dad were always invited to the high school celebration parties that most parents put on for their graduating seniors. It was not uncommon for them to attend ten to twelve graduation parties every year. This was very special to Dad taking great pride in how "his kids" had turned out. Since many of the parties were on the same day, they would hop from place to place enjoying cake, refreshments and bus stories.

Home at Last

The day Dad was released from the Nursing Home was a great day! He was so eager to be home that he could hardly contain himself. One of the conditions of his release was to show that he was able to take care of himself. This involved numerous types of occupational therapy. One of the tasks he had to perform was to be able to prepare his own breakfast. Now you must understand that my father loved breakfast. It was his favorite meal of the day and he was very particular about how he prepared his food. He jumped at the chance to show just how well he was and proceeded to the kitchen the very next morning. Having passed this task with flying colors he got the green light to leave the nursing home. We had made arrangements to pick up his walker (which by the way he hated) and be at the nursing home at 8 am the next day to help Mom transport him home. My husband and I arrived about 15 minutes early only to find Mom and Dad sitting in the front entrance. Dad had his bags next to him and his discharge papers in hand. He had had nightmares the night before dreaming that he would not be allowed to leave the facility. He was taking no chances. At the first sign of light he got dressed and insisted that the paperwork be completed immediately.

As we greeted them at the entrance, he eagerly announced, "I am now a free man, get me the heck out of here". We followed Mom as she drove Dad the short drive from Viroqua to Westby. Dad was extremely weak so it took all of us to help him out of the car and up the several steps into the house. He quickly surveyed the surroundings and gingerly moved toward his off-white leather lazy boy. Once seated he quickly stretched out and proceeded to put his feet up on the foot rest. The next thing we heard was a big sigh followed by a yawn. He was so relieved to finally be in his own home. He knew that he was blessed to be alive and be able to be in his home. Within minutes Dad was sound asleep. There would be no more clinical trial. That was okay. For now Mom and Dad would enjoy the time they had together. Things would be just fine Mom said over and over again.

We finished getting Dad's belongs in the house and then did a quick check to make sure everything else was in order. The biggest concern was the steps. Their hundred year old plus home definitely presented a problem in this area. The bedrooms were all on the second floor and the steps were extremely steep and narrow. This was how houses in that era were built and it had never been a problem for them before. The occupational therapist from the nursing had identified the problem as something that had to be dealt with prior to Dad getting released. Somehow Dad had convinced them that they would buy a hide-a-bed for the first floor and all would be fine. What they didn't know however was that Dad was adamantly opposed to this idea and was convinced that he would be able to manage the stairs.

When we took a good look at the stairs we realized that it had only one hand rail. We decided that we would go the hardware store and buy a rail and hardware. The problem was however, that we had no idea how to install the rail. We waited until Dad woke up and then positioned his lazy boy such that he could give us step-by-step directions. We giggled so hard we could hardly contain ourselves. What was such a simple task for Dad was a big deal for us. In the end we accomplished our goal. We installed the hand rail and Dad was once again feeling useful.

Even though it was summer and school was not in session during Dad's hospital and nursing home stay, he received over 500 cards and numerous visitors from his current and past bus number 7 kids. He had three generations of families praying for him and for his recovery. One boy wrote that Dad had to return to his route that fall or he would not go to school. Dad smiled when he read this proclaiming loudly that he would not let that boy down. It was obvious how proud Dad was that one of his kids felt this strongly about him.

Follow-up visits to Dr. Go were met with remarkable news. Dad's tumors were shrinking. While the cancer was not gone, there were no signs of additional tumors and no new symptoms. No one in the healthcare system could explain the turn of events other than "sometimes" things like this happened. Dad smiled and said, "That's great news. Looks like we won't be needing so many trips to the clinic from now on." As we were leaving the clinic he stopped and said he knew the real reason behind the good news; he attributed it to all the prayers said on his behalf. Mom and Dad had a very solid faith. For them God had answered their prayers.

As each day went by Dad's strength improved. The biggest problem he had was not being able to drive. Mom offered to take him wherever he wanted but this just wasn't the same. What he missed the most was his morning coffee time. He missed the comradery of about a dozen of his buddies that would meet each morning at the "Express" for coffee and conversation. Lucky for him his buddies came up with the idea to take turns coming and getting him each morning so as to not bother Mom and give Dad a little "free" time. So it was, a little after 7 am each morning the phone would ring to make sure that Dad was up to his morning outing. Within a couple of minutes a vehicle would pull into their driveway and away he went. He was glad to be back with his buddies and they were equally glad to have him back.

The next big challenge was how to handle summer vacation. Each year for roughly the past forty years Mom and Dad vacationed with friends "up north" near Hayward, Wisconsin. Mom was reluctant to go this year because she did not think Dad was strong enough and did not want to be that far away from his doctors. Dad however would not hear of it. He said that if someone could just help him hook the boat up to the back of their pickup they would be good to go. And so it was. The neighbors helped them get the boat hitched and away they went. They were both in heaven that week, enjoying the company of old friends, fishing and just hanging out. By the end of that week Dad's strength had improved a hundred fold.

The first of August came and Dad once again started to plan for the school year ahead. He had been elected President of the Bus Drivers Association and was busy meeting with drivers and administration as their contract was due. In Westby, the school buses were owned and maintained by the school district. The drivers were employees of the district and therefore had the same medical benefits as the teachers. Most of the drivers were either farmers or retired and drove bus not for the salary but for the health benefits. The teacher's health benefits were outstanding but extremely expensive for the district. This became a sticking point during the bus driver negotiations. They wanted them to take a pay cut to help offset the benefit costs.

This was sensitive issue as some districts in the area had recently outsourced both buses and the drivers to an outside company and no longer provided benefits in their package. The Westby drivers did not want this to happen so they knew they had to try to come up with something that was both acceptable to them but also acceptable to the district administration.

You need to understand something here. My Mom did not like that Dad was the head of this group. Why did Dad always need to be the leader she would say, why not settle for just being on a committee like she did. Nothing wrong with helping out versus leading she would say in her most convincing voice. Despite all her fussing, nothing changed Dad's mind or his willingness and eagerness to lead. In fact Dad was in general happiest if he was in charge. She knew that being the president of the bus drivers during this particular negotiation was going to most likely be a no win. In a small town such as Westby someone or some group was probably not going to be happy with the outcome.

Dad however was able to come up with a very creative solution to the problem at hand. Since many of the bus drivers were retirement age, they could obtain their insurance through Medicaid thus reducing the overall burden on the school district. Overall this would save the district roughly enough to fund the salary increase the drivers were looking for and allow those younger driver's to keep the school insurance. Dad discussed this proposal with his fellow bus drivers most of which thought it was a great idea. He then took the matter to the school administrator who dismissed the idea saying there were too many variables involved for this to be sustainable. Dad was very disappointed with this decision. What happened several days later however surprised him. Thanks to the visibility Dad was able to bring to the proposal the board agreed to proceed with a salary increase and continuation of benefits until further assessment could be done. The next time the topic would be on the docket would be two years from now. For now, the drivers got exactly what they were asking for.

And so their life was returning to a normal state. Dad resumed his involvement on church committees and on the planning commission for the city of Westby. Their social was back to its active state going out to dinner or playing cards with friends on a regular basis. Dad was even back golfing at the Snowflake ski club where he organized their Wednesday morning men's league fun and games.

Dad in Good Health when Tragedy Strikes

Mom and Dad's grandchild Greta was getting married in October so Mom and her girlfriend Pat were busy shopping for a special outfit for the occasion. Greta's aunt in Stoughton, near Madison had planned a bridal shower for her the third Saturday in August so all the woman in the family were busy planning for that event.

Mom was also working as a volunteer at the Beth Butikk food pantry and thrift shop in Westby. The Butikk was a store where a person of need could get food, clothing, furniture, etc. It was connected to the church and was something that Mom and her friends enjoyed doing. Mid-August of this year brought the biggest flooding the area had ever seen. The storms were relentless and many in the area were either without housing or had serious damage to their properties. It was all anyone could talk about. Mom and her friends at the Butikk were working overtime to help those in need.

The day of the wedding shower came and I offered to drive Mom and several of Greta's great aunts to the shower. Stoughton was about 3 hours away so we had a lots of girl time to discuss just about everything imaginable. I was looking forward to spending the day with Mom. The trip took us right through Viroqua and the rural areas that were so terribly devastated by the rain storms and flooding. We certainly gained a better appreciation for what many of these people were dealing with. Mom shared stories of the families that were seeking help at the Butikk. The need was great. Mom was focused and energized to be able to help.

We had a great time at the shower and even more fun when I got lost coming home. Even though I had two GPS's in the car and a truck CB, I still managed to get turned around. The ladies in the car laughed uncontrollably. Mom giggled and giggled commenting that perhaps a good old fashioned map might help. Good thing I was able to get my bearings without causing much of a delay in our return trip. As I dropped Mom off at their house in Westby I reached across the seat and gave her a big hug. This was the most time away from a medical facility I had spent with Mom in a long time and I had thoroughly enjoyed her company. Dad was working in the garage when we pulled into the driveway. He quickly dropped what he was doing running over to tell us that he had gone fishing that day and had caught his limit. He certainly was in great spirits and looked healthier than I could remember.

Dad gave Mom a big hug telling her he was happy that "his rock" was home. She was as steady as they come, no matter what kind of news they received from the Doctors, she was always convinced that they would be fine. She had read everything she could about Dad's illness. Now that they had received the good news from the Doctors she was hyper focused on helping Dad put back on the weight he had lost. The grandkids would laugh and make fun at her. They had given her the nickname of the "food pusher". She rarely sat down at a meal; instead choosing to hover over everyone in case they ran out of something or needed another helping. She was doing the same with Dad. She was preparing all his favorite dishes including dessert on a daily basis. Dad loved it. He was steadily gaining weight. Mom was convinced that within a month or so he would be back at his "pre-cancer" weight.

They were very thankful and excited to have their lives returning to normal. So normal in fact that Dad was contemplating his return to the first responder crew. He would need to be recertified which would mean several training sessions at the local Vernon Memorial hospital facility followed by skills testing. He was confident that he was ready but the challenge would be to convince Mom.

That next Monday Dad decided to talk with Mom about his plan. He was eager to return to his pager and the drama that came with being a first responder in a small town. He expected Mom to resist the idea since she was never really that excited about him being a responder. She worried about the stress of the late night calls and the pain and suffering that accompanied the calls especially in a small town where the odds were high that you would personally know the people involved or certainly knew people who were going to be affected by what was happening. She also hated the sight of blood, needles and worried about things like the aids virus. Dad reassured her that they had proper gear and training such that this would not be the case, but Mom still was concerned about this potential risk.

Dad was pleasantly surprised that rather than try to talk him out of rejoining the team she seemed genuinely ok with the idea of him becoming an active member again. She said she understood how important it was for him to be able to return to normal and knew that being a responder meant a great deal to him.

Dad called me that evening to tell me the good news. I would guess it was kind of like how it was with the lawn mowing task. When Dad first came home from the hospital Mom insisted on mowing the lawn, something that Dad had always done and enjoyed doing in the past. She mowed the lawn with the exception of the boulevard which was too difficult for Mom to manage. As Dad's strength improved so did his desire to mow the yard. As the argument over who would mow became more and more intense, Mom shared the story with her good friend Pat. Pat proceeded to tell Mom that maybe this was something that Dad really needed to do to help him know that he was in fact becoming his normal self. My guess is that this was in the back of her mind as she listened to Dad tell her about his desire to return to the first responder team. Dad loved being a part of that team and deep down Mom knew that this too was a part of him regaining his independence.

A refresher CPR class was being held that Wednesday at the Viroqua hospital, so Dad decided that would be a great time to rejoin the group. Mom was going to meet her friends for afternoon coffee but decided instead to make Dad an apple pie. She wanted to make sure that when he returned that evening from his training he would have something special and of course substantial for his bedtime snack.

She had been working in the basement most of the day sorting through old clothes, furniture and unused household items. She was sorting them into piles so that Dad could take them to the "Butikk" the next morning. I talked with Dad about 5:00 pm. He was very excited about the evening ahead. Mom was busy making dinner so she could not come to the phone. As was usually the case I could hear her talking in the background; most of the time correcting or adding to what Dad was saying. They had a great relationship which included Mom gently poking at Dad on a routine basis. It was delightful to hear them both in such good humor.

Six and a half hours later there was loud pounding on our front door. Someone was ringing the doorbell over and over again. Having just talked with Mom and Dad we had turned the phone off before going to sleep and as usual closed our bedroom door. Who could possibly be at our door at this time of the night?

My husband told me to stay in bed and went downstairs to see who was at the door. I heard muted male voices and then looked up to see my husband's shadow in the hall. I knew from his posture that something terrible had happened. By this time I was wide awake.

Your Mom has had an accident explained the stone faced chaplain; after which I was sure he would say and she was in the hospital. Instead, after a short pause, he said, "and she died". She died! I couldn't believe it. I had just heard her voice. Just last Saturday we had spent the entire day together. Mom and Dad looked very happy as they stood together waving at me as I left their house just this past Saturday. I glanced over to the police officer who was standing next to the chaplain and knew from the look on his face that what he said was true. The two of them had traveled together to deliver this devastating news. I asked what happened and the officer slowly, almost painstakingly, said that Mom had fallen. August 29, 2007, they estimate sometime around 7 pm my Mom had fallen down the basement steps and died.

Dad had returned home immediately following the first responder training and sat down to enjoy a piece of the apple pie Mom had made. It was just about 9 pm somewhere between dusk and darkness. The house was quiet so Dad assumed Mom had gone upstairs to bed as she sometimes did when

Dad was later than 8 pm. Dad was about to take his last couple of bites of apple pie when he noticed that the door to the basement was open and the downstairs light was on. He got up to turn the light off and shut the door when he glanced to the bottom of the stairs and saw Mom.

There she lay, flat on her back in her nightgown at the bottom of the stairs. She was bleeding from her ears, eyes, nose and mouth. She had a huge black and blue bulge next to her right eye. Dad knew that she had taken a serious fall. Dad's first responder training kicked in and he did his best to administer CPR. He knew however deep in his heart that it was too late. He had seen trauma like this before and knew that there was really nothing more that could be done. She had lost an enormous amount of blood and was unconscious. He ran up the stairs and called 911. The operator told him that the first responders were unavailable that evening due to training and told Dad that the hospital would be called but it might be a little bit before the ambulance would be there. Dad who is rarely abrupt told the person on the other end of the phone that the training was in fact over and to page the responders immediately.

A Westby police officer, also a friend of Mom and Dad's was there immediately. The first responders, all of them, arrived within minutes and were doing their best to try to save Mom. They administered CPR, performed a tracheotomy, inserted a chest tube and started an IV. I later learned from the head EMT, one of Mom and Dad's closest friends, that while all the people at the site knew that Mom was already dead, they still proceeded to do everything they possibly could medically to try to revive her. This they did this as much for themselves as they did for Dad. Dad had called Pastor Julie, who happened to live only a couple of blocks away. Her husband, also a Pastor answered the phone and told Dad that Julie had already gone to bed. When Dad told him what had happened, he said not to worry, that she would be there in a couple of minutes. She actually ran the couple of blocks to the house and arrived in time to say a prayer for Mom and Dad and ride with Mom in the ambulance. Dad rode with the police officer trailing close behind the ambulance.

Mom never regained consciousness. The emergency room doctor pronounced her dead on arrival. That was it. In a matter of minutes her life was gone. Dad had been trying to call us but to no avail. Finally the Westby police officer had notified the La Crosse police department and that is how the officer and chaplain made their way to our house.

The police officer was fumbling with his shirt pocket as though looking for something. Finally he took out a piece of paper with a phone number for me to call. I dialed the number and waited for someone to answer. At this point everything appeared to be happening in slow motion. The person on the other end of the phone was the receptionist in the emergency ward. I told her I was the daughter of Ilene Ekern and needed to talk with my father. There was a short pause followed by a shuffling noise. Dad was the next voice I heard. Hey Toots, he said sounding remarkably calm. Mom took a fall and didn't make it. We did everything we could but it was too late. The tone of his voice suddenly softened and quivered ever so little as he proceeded to ask if I wanted to see Mom before they took her away. I told him we would be right there.

The forty five minute drive from our house to the hospital seemed like an eternity. The night was extremely hot and humid. The air was thick and seemed to be doing its best to suffocate anything or everyone in its path. I however was shivering uncontrollably for the entire drive. We pulled into the emergency room parking lot and noticed my older brother's truck illegally parked at the entrance. The automatic doors swung open followed by an intense flood of cold conditioned air. My Dad rushed to hug me. The next thing I remember were the tears. We cried together and held each other for what seemed like several minutes.

When I finally a looked at Dad's eyes I saw the horrible pain and hurt he was enduring. Dad's eyes were swollen, bloodshot and as glassy as a lake just before sunset. We both took a breath and walked hand-in-hand to the waiting room. My brother Reid, his wife Nancy, Pastor Julie and Mom and Dad's best friend, Bob and Gloria were huddled together in the small waiting room. The atmosphere was solemn as my sister-in-law and Gloria sat quietly compiling a list of people who should be notified. Pastor Julie was quick to provide comforting words, but no matter how hard she tried, the words did not help. Dad then asked if I was ready to see Mom. I nodded my head yes, even though the rest of my body and mind said no.

We followed the nurse to one of the patient rooms. Dad held my hand and squeezed it so hard that my attention was taken away from what I was about to see. There she was, prone on a metal cart, wrapped in hospital blankets. I stood at her side and kissed her forehead. Dad held my hand and told me everything would be ok. She was cold and so battered. Her bloodied black and blue face was now bloated and distorted. Pastor Julie said a quick prayer and that was it. There was nothing more to say or do.

The hospital staff gave us a gift as we left that night. I thought it odd at the time, but later as Dad opened the box I realized the comfort provided to Dad by the inscription commemorating life. I guess that is the beauty of being a part of a small community. When there is a tragedy, everyone comes to your aid; everyone cares.

Dad rode with us the short distance to Mom and Dad's house. The basement floor carpet where Mom had landed was covered in blood. For whatever reason we all, Dad, my brother and myself felt compelled to try and get rid of the blood that night. We sat together in the basement taking turns blotting blood from the carpet using vinegar water and old towels. I guess there must have been something therapeutic about trying to rid ourselves of the blood, the memory of the fall and the loss of Mom. We did our best to erase the events of the evening; but to no avail.

The phone rang about an hour after we returned from the hospital. I answered and was surprised to hear the voice on the other end of the phone identify himself as the supervisor of the hospital morgue. In a very matter of fact manner he proceeded to tell me they had taken Mom to the morgue, cleaned her up and wanted us to know that she was doing just fine. Doing just fine, I thought to myself. She is dead, how can she be fine! I was appalled. I could not believe what this guy had just told me. I stormed downstairs to relay the message to Dad. Much to my surprise Dad was relieved by the news. He was glad to know that she was being so well cared for. It was at that point that I was once again reminded of how incredible my father was. He had the amazing ability to be positive in the most adverse situations.

About an hour later, my baby brother Todd arrived. He lives in Rockford, Illinois and had gotten there as fast as he could. He had not wanted to see Mom so he came directly to the house. I marveled at Dad's strength. When Todd came, he proceeded to tell him the entire story being careful to cover every detail. Todd absorbed as best could and proceeded to join in on the cleanup effort. He was the one that told us we probably needed to get some sleep before the activities of the day ahead completely consumed us. He also suggested that tomorrow we try using the wetvac to get rid of the remaining blood stains. Funny what people do and say in stressful situations.

Todd was staying with Dad so we went home to try and get some sleep. For me, sleep would not come. Instead I played the piano. While we did not have a lot of money growing up Mom and Dad had seen to it that we had piano lessons. Reid who was two years older than me quit taking lessons the day I passed him in the lesson book. We used to play duets together. "The Beautiful Danube" was my Mom's favorite. She loved to hear us play. Randy, who was two years younger than me had the gift of "playing by ear". That meant that a song that may have taken me a couple of weeks to learn, he could just sit down and play. That left me as the only piano student. Seventeen years of lessons provided me with ample experience and musical knowledge. I played regularly at church and for school activities.

Mom loved to hear me play. She said she could tell what kind of mood I was in by the way I played a song. Tonight I played for her. I played and played and cried harder than ever before. I knew Mom was listening to me play and prayed for peace and calm. I knew that I wanted to play something for Mom's funeral so began searching for just the right song.

Morning couldn't come soon enough. By 7:30 am we were on our way back to Westby.

Dad had just finished breakfast and Todd was working on the carpet when we arrived. Randy, my brother who was living in St. Louis was flying in this morning and would be at the house around 10 am.

Dad and I sat at the dinner table and began to talk about Mom's funeral. I was surprised by how strong an opinion Dad had about the service. He listed off the names of the men he wanted as pallbearers, what kind of service he wanted and exactly what kind of food he wanted at the luncheon following the funeral. He knew that he wanted their dear friend Fritz to sing and asked me to take the first cut at the obituary.

Dad had requested an autopsy so that we would know for sure if Mom had died accidentally from the fall or if she had perhaps suffered a heart attack prior to the fall. Dad had made arrangements with the funeral home to transport Mom's body to Madison where this would be conducted. In addition he requested that as many of Mom's organs and body parts as was possible be donated knowing that this would be her wishes. They had had many discussions about this topic among themselves and friends and both felt strongly about the positive impact one could have on another person even after they were no longer on this earth.

We were set to meet with the funeral director at 1 pm that afternoon. I busied myself on the computer trying without much success to draft Mom's obituary while Dad answered the nonstop phone calls. Shortly after 8:15 am an elderly neighbor lady, whom Mom and Dad rarely saw or talked with came to the door and asked for Mom. Dad told her that she wasn't there. The lady proceeded to ask when she would be there. Dad explained that she had died the night before. He closed the door and started to sob. She would never be back he said over and over again. The reality of the situation was starting to sink in.

Although it was less than twelve hours since Mom's accident, word of her death had travelled fast. At precisely 9 am it was as though the flood gates opened. A steady stream of people flowed through the house. The closest of friends and family arriving through the back door armed with sandwiches, jello molds and hot dish casseroles. Through the front door a flood of neighbors, bus families, coworkers, and friends, too many to count bearing fruit baskets, cheese trays and well wishes. A first responder friend who stayed behind at the house when they took Mom by ambulance had taken a quick inventory of things we might need at the house knowing that most likely they were not going to be able to resuscitate Mom. She proceeded to bring coffee, paper products and other staples to the house so we would not need to concern ourselves with such matters. Another close friend arranged for meals to be brought to the house for the next several days and dropped off a notebook so that we could keep track of who was bringing what allowing for an easier time when it came time to write thank you notes. It was amazing to experience the outpouring of love and support. I found it interesting though that people want and need to "do something" during a time like this versus just being there.

Painstakingly, Dad replayed the events of the past evening to each group of people that arrived. Randy arrived mid-morning and listened intently as Dad described what had happened. It must have been Dad's way of dealing with the situation but for me listening to the details over and over again, was almost too much to bear.

Before we knew it was time to go to the mortuary. Mom's body was not yet back from Madison but we proceeded to make the arrangements for the visitation and funeral. I was a bit overwhelmed as this was the first time I had been a part of this process. The mortician was a friend of the family which should have made this easier however he started talking about the autopsy, organ and tissue donation and before long I was sobbing uncontrollably. Again Dad took this all in stride seeming to appreciate knowing the details about what was happening. Dad picked out the casket and vault; choosing conservative as we all knew that that is what Mom would have wanted (she was rather frugal to say the least).

He also outlined for Pastor Julie what he wanted for the funeral service. Within 45 minutes the entire process was complete. We still needed to complete the obituary and pick out the clothes for Mom to wear, but other than that everything was set.

Both these items were clearly in my court and I knew that putting these tasks off was not going to make them easier. Through tears and sobs the first draft of the obituary was complete. Now it was up to Dad and brothers to add, delete or modify as they thought fit. My sister-in-law escorted me up to Mom's closet to help me pick out something appropriate for Mom to wear. This was tough. Mom was not a fancy person so I knew that she would want to be buried in something simple yet classy. I chose three outfits deciding to let Dad make the final choice. Brown, he though, too drab; Yellow, not his favorite color. Red; yes that was it. He had made his selection. I decided to wait to pick out the jewelry until the next day.

Throughout that entire day the house was a buzz with well-wishers. Many of Dad's past and current bus "kids" came to the house with food, hugs and words of comfort. One little boy, a first grader was extremely curious about what had happened and was eager to talk to Dad about the details. Despite the best efforts of his Mom and Dad to curtail his curiosity, he proceeded to ask the questions that were on his mind. "Richard, is it true that your wife fell down the stairs? Show me where this happened? Is she really dead? Another little girl wanted to know if Dad was really going to put her body in the ground and put dirt on top of her. Without skipping a beat, Dad answered all their questions and even showed him the steps where Mom had fallen. Dad was oddly comforted by this straightforward approach and knew that the honesty and innocence of his bus kids would be a great strength to him in the days to come.

Late in the day while Dad was spending time with two of their closest couples, the phone rang. I was working on the latest revisions to the obituary when I heard Dad's voice answer the phone. I went into the kitchen just in time to hear him thank the coroner for calling so quickly. Dad hung up the phone and reluctantly told me that the autopsy was complete. There had been no heart attack or other medical condition. Mom had merely fallen and died as a result. The official cause of death was now known; she died of a traumatic head injury. For me the news was devastating. My secret hope was that she had died of a heart attack and then fallen. Somehow in my mind, I thought this would have been less painful. The thought of my Mother falling and then laying on the basement floor to die was beyond my comprehension. Now I had to face the truth. Dad did his best to reassure me that she did not suffer. Based on his first responder experience, the extent of her injuries, and the position of her body he was certain that death had been instantaneous. He said that she was lying on her back, with her feet crossed and arms at her side. There were no signs of a struggle. Her glasses and watch were on her nightstand in the upstairs bedroom. As best we can figure she had gone to bed and then realized that she had left a light on in the basement. She went to the basement to turn off the light and then fell. The facts were clear. Mom was gone. There was nothing we could do to bring her back to us.

Our job now was to support Dad. He tirelessly planned every detail of Mom's funeral assuring that she would be remembered with the respect and dignity she deserved. We assembled numerous picture boards depicting the importance of family and friends in her life and took them to the funeral home for people to view during the visitation. The granddaughters were singing a song with me accompanying on the piano and Mom's dear friend had written a poem to be read at the funeral. Dad had finalized the obituary and in lieu of flowers he requested that memorials be given to the church for a new kitchen floor or to the Bethel Butikk. The Butikk was in desperate need of funding given the strain the flooding had taken on the region. The kitchen floor had long been a source of frustration for Mom. She and her friends spent countless hours in the kitchen preparing and serving meals and fund raisers for the church. The original floor was uneven concrete and caused many of the women to have leg and back pain by the end of a day's work. Dad was pleased with the choices for memorials and was hopeful that Mom's memorials would make a significant contribution to the overall costs.

When the time came for the visitation to begin the Pastor met with the immediate family for a brief prayer and meditation. Just as the pastor was about to finish Dad began to fidget. He cleared his throat and began to stand turning around to make eye contact and shared his expectations for the next several days. We were to "host" the events of the next several days. There would be a great many people coming to pay their respects and he wanted to make sure that we did our best to welcome people and to "mingle". "This was not a time for us to huddle together in a corner and wait for people to approach us", Dad said in a very matter of a fact fashion much like the sound of Mom's firm voice we had all grown accustomed to over the years. It was apparent that Dad felt strongly about this and as a result we all did our best to carry out his wishes.

The visitation was set to last three hours, but went well into the fourth hour do to the large number of people in attendance. While many people knew that Dad had been very ill and that his prognosis was not good; the news of Mom's fall and sudden death came as a huge shock. The entire town was in mourning; in fact as one of my Mom's best friends said, "All of Vernon County was in mourning". Another of Dad's bus kid mom's reminded us that "the real mourning starts when the last casserole dish is returned", with a not so subtle reminder that if we need support we should be sure to reach out. Their community of friends was there for us.

Cancer Returns but First We Must Honor Mom

The Saturday of Labor Day weekend 2007 was the day we buried Mom. The weather was warm, humid and mostly sunny. High white clouds whisked across the sky. How surreal. Less than a week ago the region was engulfed in storms and flooding. On this day most of the physical traces of the storm were gone except for the rock cliffs between the bluffs and valleys. A gentle stream of water continued to seep out of the hillside; glistening in the sunshine. For me it was as though even nature was mourning my mother's loss.

Dad took great care getting dressed that morning knowing that Mom would want him to look his very best. Dad had lost a considerable amount of weight since his hospital stay so I had picked up a new outfit for him to wear; complete with several ties. The grandchildren would get the final say on which one to wear; so as to make sure he looked "with it".

He was upstairs getting dressed when I heard him call for me. I assumed that he needed help with his tie. I quickly reminded him that we didn't have a lot of time to be messing around. It was time to get to the church. When I got to their bedroom, he was staring at himself in the mirror with his hand touching his neck. It was then that he shared the real reason for asking me upstairs. He had discovered several new lymph nodes protruding from his neck. Neither of us said a word. We both knew what this meant. The cancer was back. We hugged each other and agreed that it was time for us to go. Dad said that today was not about him; but instead a day to remember Mom. He finished tying his tie and we both nodded in approval. He straightened his shoulders and adjusted his tie one final time. Perfect...Mom would have certainly approved.

The funeral itself was a blur. The church was packed. Over four hundred people packed the pews. Dad walked with slow and deliberate steps as we entered the church. He was determined to be strong. The suggestion to perhaps use a walker or cane fell on deaf ears. As we processed behind the casket, he carefully acknowledged as many people as he could giving special attention to his many school bus kids. His bus kids came in many shapes and sizes, some being current riders and many being past riders. The current riders were young and very impressionable; most accompanied by their parents. It was obvious that for most of them this was the first funeral they had ever attended. His tears and sobs barely subdued by the organ music. The past riders, many who were now parents themselves paid careful attention to every move Dad made. It was as though Dad was a father to each one of them. You could see the empathy and compassion they felt for Dad and could feel how badly they wanted to try to make things "normal" once again.

Most of Dad's kids did not have the kind of personal relationship with Mom as with Dad, but they certainly felt as though they knew her well. For the past forty years, Mom and Dad had attended almost every musical concert and many of the school sporting events. Together they had cheered and applauded the accomplishments of Dad's bus kids. She was also known for the many notes and cards she had sent over the years. She made sure that a personal handwritten note was always sent in the event of a family hardship or illness. Although behind the scenes, the bus kids certainly knew how much Mom meant to Dad.

We settled into our seats and listened carefully as Pastor Julie presided over the service. The Bible verses and the sermon focused on the power of believing and provided several parallels to floods, disasters, and Mom's accident.

Dad had requested that the congregation sing one of Mom and Dad's favorite church songs, entitled, "You Have Come Down to the Lakeshore" by Cesareo Gabarain. Mom especially liked the refrain.

> *Sweet Lord, you have looked into my eyes, kindly smiling, you've called out my name. On the sand I have abandoned my small boat; now with you, I will seek other seas.*

About two years earlier during a sing along at our house, our family gathered around the piano as Mom and Dad taught us this hymn. It was a new hymn in their church and they wanted to share it with the rest of the family. In jest, Dad said that he wanted it sung at his funeral. Mom, being the sentimental-quick-to tears person was just about to unleash a flood gate of tears when Dad reached over and gave her a quick hug. We all giggled and tried to sway back and forth as we concentrated on the unfamiliar rhythm. Not a traditional Lutheran hymn Dad remarked. This of course evoked another round of laughter as Mom encouraged us to try to harmonize with the melody. Mom and Dad often sang together and many times managed to harmonize their voices. Fortunately they shared this love of music with their children and grandchildren. We worked on this song for almost an hour that day until Mom was happy with the harmony and was assured that the tempo and rhythm were just right.

How ironic that less than two years later we would be doing our best to bring justice to this song in Mom's honor. As the organist did her best to bring a modern quick-paced tempo to the song, the congregation tentatively sang the words. During the first two verses Dad and I found it too difficult to sing. The lump in our throats was almost unbearable. Then as though prompted by Mom, Dad clutched my hand and began to harmonize. I leaned in as close as I could to Dad and together we managed to create beautiful harmony for the last two versus. We knew by the end of the song that Mom was certainly watching over us. We knew that if she had anything to say about it, everything was going to be just fine.

Mom loved music and throughout the years was known by the grandkids to gather us around the piano while I accompanied singing all her favorite songs. The granddaughters decided it would be fitting to sing at Mom's funeral. So, with me on the piano they chose to sing a song entitled "I'll Fly Away" as a tribute. The song is an old gospel spiritual. The lyrics are as follows:

> *Some glad morning when this life is o'er, I'll fly away. To a home on God's celestial shore, I'll fly away. I'll fly away, O glory, I'll fly away. When I die, hallelujah, by and by, Oh I'll fly away.*

Just a few more weary days and then, I'll fly away. To a land where joy shall never end, I'll fly away. I'll fly away, O glory, I'll fly away. When I die, hallelujah, by and by, Oh I'll fly away.

Dad said that he knew Mom would like the song as it was very upbeat. As we practiced, we could almost hear Mom encouraging us to stand tall, enunciate, project, and to be sure to give it a big finish. Mom was always giving "gentle reminders" to Dad and the rest of us kids and grandkids about how to behave. Heaven forbid if she should ever have to use her "firm voice" or call out (in her high pitched shriek voice) R-i-c-h-a-r-d! Everyone in the family knew, Dad included, that we had better shape up, immediately. Dad smiled as we finished the song knowing that Mom would have loved the song and would have been even more pleased by how well we had performed it. Yes, Dad was right. She would have loved it.

When the time came to leave the church, Dad clenched my hand and struggled to steady himself. He was obviously weak and the neuropathy in his feet (a side effect of the chemotherapy) was flaring its ugly head. As we followed the casket down the center isle all eyes were upon us. Dad did his best to remain composed; there was not a dry eye in the entire church.

The motorcade to the gravesite was slow and deliberate. The winding country road was filled with every make and model car with family and friends who wanted to help lay Mom to rest. Dad had asked a very close friend to drive the hearse. I watched in amazement as Dad moved forward to help the pallbearers lift Mom's body and casket into the vehicle. It was at that moment that he noticed Pastor Julie. She had conducted Mom's service with such calm and control. Now, in this relatively private moment she began to cry. Dad was the first to comfort her. His unselfish demeanor was so predictable. He knew the power of a strong hug and a couple of soft spoken words. Within minutes everything was back on track and we were all proceeding to the cemetery.

Mom and Dad had purchased their burial plots several years earlier. Together with several of their closest friends they had methodically selected plots in a newer less populated area of the cemetery. They did this so that they could all be buried close to each other. As odd as this seemed to me; Mom, Dad and their friends really did not seem this was unusual. Their friends were very important to them. Knowing that they would be near even in death provided them comfort. Mom had even made it clear to us kids as well as their close friends that she was to be buried to Dad's right, on the inside, farthest away from the road. She said she did not want to be bothered with traffic. So as she had wished, we buried her in the plot furthest from the road.

Mom and Dad had also debated, sometimes in jest and sometimes in an unusual seriousness what type of graveside monument or headstone they would have at their burial site. Mom wanted a traditional monument. She would have a polished granite, preferably black, perhaps deep grey stone complete with neatly engraved names, dates and some kind of profound inscription. Nothing too large or extravagant, but rather something classy.

Dad on the other hand wanted to "create" a monument. That's right, he wanted their headstone to be a unique one of a kind never to be duplicated work of art. His vision was to find two rocks with features representing their personalities. His would be a strong solid rock with slightly rough edges. Moms would be a smaller more petite yet still formidable rock with more refined edges. Dad would place the rocks upright by affixing them to deep burgundy colored concrete and have custom plaques designed with minimal personal information.

With Dad's health issues progressing as they were, we were quite sure Mom would be the one to decide the fate of their headstones. Now, with Mom's sudden death, Dad was left to make the final decision. He mentioned this to me the day we were picking out the casket but we decided that the task at hand was overwhelming enough. He would have plenty of time to decide this at a later date. Even though he had consciously put off the discussion for another time, it was obvious that

Dad's mind was busy mulling over the options. Perhaps he should do something traditional knowing that was what Mom would have done; or perhaps she would be disappointed if he hadn't done what he had talked of doing. Over and over the options would play. Finally just about the time that the Pastor was reciting the ashes to ashes, dust to dust part, I felt a calm come over Dad. He took my hand in his and gently whispered in my ear that the creative option would be best. Mom would want him to carry on with his plans. He was sure of it. I noticed a look of resolve and knew that this topic would not be discussed again.

The air was still and calm as people hugged and kissed my dad offering condolences before returning to their cars and going back to the church for the reception. Purposefully, I wished time to stand still. If sheer will alone could have slowed the universe; at that moment there would have been a not so subtle pause. I was not ready to leave my Mom. In fact I was never going to be ready to leave Mom. Dad placed a flower on the casket and then in a very matter of fact fashion went on to explain how the cemetery caretakers would lower Mom's casket into the ground and seal the vault as soon as we left. He went on the say that they would then fill the grave with black dirt, take care to level the site and then scatter a type of fast growing grass seed on the top soil. He was sure that by late fall grass would be growing and that only slight leveling and minor reseeding would be needed by spring.

This entire message was spoken with a kind of confidence and self-assuredness that only my Dad could do. True to form, always being the caretaker. He knew stuff; always had and always would.

As we went through the funeral process, there were several items that I just didn't understand and/or appreciate. I shared my concerns with Dad but he quickly clarified why things are typically done as they are and why it was important to him to stay with tradition.

First, I didn't understand why he felt so strongly about an open casket. Mom's head and face had taken the brunt of her fall. Even the hands of a skilled mortician could not recreate her likeness. Dad however was adamant that if at all possible the viewing should include an open casket. He said that it helped people come to terms with the fact that she was dead.

The same was true for the visitation. I viewed this as an unnecessary strain on the family. Again, he came down on the side of all the friends, relative, neighbors and coworkers that would want to pay their respects. Again he felt that it was a good way for people to come to terms with the loss.

Finally, I really didn't get the idea of a luncheon after the funeral. The last thing that I wanted to do was to eat something. Dad insisted that this type of fellowship was just what people including our family needed. A time to focus on the good times, share stories and help each other know that everything was going to be ok. He was a positive upbeat person who took life in stride. Little did I know that having this knowledge would become very pertinent and helpful when it came time to deal with Dad's passing.

As soon as most of the people had left the luncheon we proceeded to pack up the leftovers, thank the ladies who had prepared and served the meal and return to Mom and Dad's house. It was later in the day by then and everyone was exhausted. There was a flurry of activity as everyone changed into casual clothes and gathered in lawn chairs on the front yard. The fresh air was delightful. Several of the Number 7 Bus families stopped by seeing we were gathered on the front lawn expressing their support to Dad for any upcoming help he may need. Everything from bringing evening meals, to helping with laundry, cleaning and/or running errands was offered. It was obvious that they were going to take good care of Dad in the days and months that followed.

One of Mom's favorite drinks was Asti Spumate. She made sure that at holidays and other special events we would take time to toast each other with a glass or two of the bubbly. Tonight would be no different. We took a couple of chilled bottles from the extra refrigerator in the garage and carried them onto the front porch near the lawn where everyone was sitting. In celebratory fashion we uncorked the Asti and toasted Mom just as the sun was setting. As dusk gave way to darkness, stars filled the sky. Mom was shining down on us, we were sure of it. We were confident she was pleased with the events of the day.

Time to Address Cancer AGAIN

The week following Mom's funeral we wrote hundreds of thank you notes as well as meeting with Dad's oncologist and radiologist. Multiple lymph nodes were now protruding from Dad's neck. The recommendation from Dr. Go and his colleagues was an aggressive round of radiation; forty days' worth to be precise. Dad said, "bring it on…sooner was better than later", and so the treatments began! He had an insatiable desire to live and was eager to do whatever it took to make sure that this was the case.

In addition to writing thank you notes and going to Doctor appointments, he was eager to giveaway Mom's clothes and other personal things. He asked that I go through her things and give as much as possible to the Bethel Butikk. I believe his motives were two fold. First, the boutique was in dire need of woman's clothes and other accessories since the recent flood. Second and I believe the primary driver was that Dad could not bear seeing her things throughout the house. He was very much a realist and knew that she would not be coming back. The sooner someone less fortunate could benefit from Mom's things the better. Within two weeks, virtually all of Mom's clothes and personal effects were disposed of. He was pleased with how quickly we were able to accomplish this and was especially pleased to know that some of his most needy Bus families were able to benefit from the donated items.

The target of Dad's radiation treatments was on his throat and upper chest. He was outfitted with a form fitting plastic mask for his face and chest. This allowed the technicians to bolt the mask to the table thus aligning his head and shoulders to be in the same position for each treatment. At first Dad felt claustrophobic as the mask and restrictive position were very confining, but knew he did not have a lot of options. He said he would just have to tough it out; and so he did. There was no complaining; in fact not another word was said about the actual treatment procedure.

The end of that first week brought about another significant event. The school year was about to begin. We as a family were reluctant to have

Dad return to driving given all he had been through, both physically and emotionally. Our words however fell on deaf ears. Dad was bound and determined to drive his route again this year. His boss suggested a substitute for the first week or so but again Dad would not hear of it. He desperately wanted to return to some sort of normalcy and knew that the support of his Bus Number 7 kids and their families was just what he needed. Nothing was going to stop him from being behind the wheel of "his Bus Number 7".

We met the first day of school with great apprehension. Dad however was eager and confident that it was the right thing to do. As it turned out Dad was right. The day was filled with an outpouring of love and affection. Children accompanied by one or both of their parents waited at the end of their driveways to give Dad hugs, kisses and encouragement. They were as excited and eager to see Dad as he was them. He was overwhelmed by the compassion of the children. He knew then and there his Bus Number 7 kids would be critical to his making it through the next several months. He knew this was going to be a very special year.

As he approached the end of his route that first day, he pulled up to the house of a little third-grade girl. He noticed that contrary to the excitement most of the kids had displayed this little girl waited patiently for him to arrive. She approached the bus with her head down and her hands at her side. Dad opened the doors only to find the little girl with tears streaming down her face. Dad put the bus in neutral and quickly moved to her side to see what was wrong. She could hardly speak. Finally as her eyes met Dad's she muttered, "I'm so sorry for your loss Richard," and then burst into tears. Realizing that she did not quite know how to handle the situation, Dad reassured her that everything was going to be fine and offered to have her sit right behind him for the remainder of the route. Since this was a spot Dad usually reserved for the very youngest and least experienced riders on his bus, she was visibly pleased by his gesture. Dad was deeply touched by her sincerity and from that moment on they formed a lasting bond.

It was at this point that Dad realized that not only did driving bus give him a reason for getting up in the morning it was providing him another reason for living. He knew that he meant a great deal to his Bus Number 7 kids. On this day he also understood how special they were to him. He was going to do his very best not let them down. He was on mission to conquer cancer and to be there for his kids.

Every weekday for the next four weeks Dad endured radiation treatments. He scheduled the treatments so that for the most part he would not need a substitute to drive his bus. He would drive his usual route in the morning, get done in time to drive the 35 miles to La Crosse, have his treatment and then drive the 35 miles back to Westby. His goal was to be back in time to drive his evening route.

Being a first responder, Dad knew most all the policemen in the area. He was confident that on those occasions where a little additional speed was needed in order to get back in time to drive his route he would not be stopped. In the event that someone inadvertently stopped him, he was confident that they would provide a personal escort. The only officers he worried about were the state patrol. Luckily he was never picked up.

We also learned by accident that Dad actually did have a backup plan. His supervisor who oversaw the bus drivers and maintenance of the buses had agreed to take Dad's route in the event that he not show up in time. If Dad was running late his boss would personally drive the bus from the garage up to the bus line at the school. This would give Dad a good extra fifteen minutes of valuable time. Dad was grateful for the support and frequently offered to take extra-curricular bus trips to return the favor. Dad was an extremely conscientious employee and wanted to make sure that he was pulling his weight and not receiving any special treatment. When we asked why he had not shared this, he smiled and said that "he liked building a little suspense into the equation!"

The radiation treatments to Dad's neck and upper chest were physically very demanding. The Doctor had warned us that Dad's skin could be "burned" in the process of the radiation. What we had not anticipated was how serious and painful this would actually be. His skin was severely burned. As time wore on we realized that those initial words by the Doctor were a serious understatement. The skin on Dad's neck, back and chest blistered, peeled and blistered and peeled over and over again. His throat became so sore that he was unable to eat solid foods. His weight was falling fast. He was surviving on "Ensure" and ice cream shakes from Culvers.

In addition to the burns and pain from radiation, he continued to experience major problems with diarrhea. After trying numerous home remedies, complete with a shot of blackberry brandy every night (this was a big deal since Dad did not drink) we decided that we were dealing with a more serious health issue.

The hospital and clinic had recently assigned us a "patient advocate". This was a rather new position within the healthcare system, charged with the job of coordinating and interpreting complicated medical cases between the patient and medical staff. Dad called her, "Our gal at Gunderson". Her insights and knowledge proved to be invaluable.

When she learned of Dad's reoccurring problem with diarrhea, she arranged to have him tested for a condition called C-Diff. The test confirmed that he was suffering from a bacterial infection. We later learned that this type of infection was quite common in people who have been on high dose antibiotics and/or spent long periods of time in the hospital or nursing home. Dad had experienced all of these things. To combat the infection he was once again put on a strong round of antibiotics. Several weeks passed with little or no improvement. His body was in serious trouble. The effects of the radiation coupled with severe diarrhea were taking a toll.

Throughout this ordeal however Dad remained remarkably optimistic. Not only did he not miss a day of driving bus he also decided he was going to go on a mission trip to Mexico. For the past couple of years friends of Dad and Mom's, Dick and Geri, went to Mexico with a team of people who examined and fit people in the region with eye glasses. Each year

Dad had sent along a hand-crafted wooden rocking horse to be given to the children of a local orphanage. Many times they had been invited along for the trip but Mom was always reluctant to go. She was not typically the adventurous type. Dad however loved new experiences and had really always wanted to go. This was the epitome of compromise within a marriage. For over fifty years they had weathered the give and take of sharing a life together. This was just one example of where Dad comprised to accommodate Mom's preference.

Now with Mom's passing things were different. Dad really wanted to go and decided that there was no time like the present to take advantage of this opportunity. He was excited to go with the group and was especially eager to hand deliver his rocking horse. He knew that some might think he was moving ahead too quickly. His philosophy however was different. Dad and Mom had a great relationship. He knew that she would want him to get on about the job of living and not sit around wallowing in his sorrow. So, after talking this over with Pastor Julie and us he decided he would go. He was ecstatic. The group was leaving in three weeks. He would be done with the radiation and was confident that if he could get the diarrhea under he would be good to go. A cousin of Mom's, Lorena, recommended trying probiotics to help with diarrhea. Much to our surprise it worked. He was now more determined than ever to make the trip.

That is when he realized he would need a passport. Although too late to go through traditional channels, Dad was quick to come up with an alternative plan. Dad was a problem solver. Give him a problem and he would find a solution. As a result of personal connections, several of which were former Bus Number 7 riders, he was able to go directly to the County seat for the application. In a matter of a week had his passport in hand. His spirits were in high gear.

The day after his last radiation treatment we decided to celebrate. My husband and I made arrangements to meet Dad in Stoddard, a little town on the Mississippi River for a pan fishing outing. Mom and Dad loved to fish and spent many days and evenings with friends fishing in this area.

We were meeting Dad after his morning bus run and would be done in time for him to drive his evening route. We arrived at the boat landing about ten minutes before Dad. The weather was gorgeous. The air was a bit crisp but we knew that by noon it would be a picture-perfect day. We were busy getting our gear ready when we saw Dad pull into the boat landing with his fishing boat on a trailer behind his pick-up truck. We waved and motioned for him to start backing into the landing. Instead of responding to us, he stopped in the middle of the road. We knew from the expression on his face that something was not right. While driving the bus route the night before he experienced a slight pain in his right groin. When he got home that evening he took off his clothes and noticed a growth. He had called Dr. Go early that morning and was told to come to the clinic as soon as he could. As usual he drove bus and then came to tell us the news. Ever the eternal optimist he brought the boat with just in case it turned out to be nothing! After all he certainly did not want to waste a great fall day if he didn't have to.

So, rather than going fishing we followed Dad to the clinic. Dr. Go had ordered a CAT-scan so we picked up the orders and proceeded to the floor where this procedure was to be performed. We were all too familiar with the clinic by this time and quickly found our way. Luckily we were the only ones in the waiting room. We were all thankful that Dad was able to get in so quickly. We were even more thankful that there was no time to chit-chat; trying to avoid any discussion about what the problem was. "The sooner we knew what we were dealing with the better", my optimistic father said. Within an hour and a half of entering the clinic we received the diagnosis. Cancer, this time appearing in the groin area.

That evening he came to terms with the fact that this new diagnosis would prevent him from going to Mexico. In typical fashion he shrugged his shoulders and said, "Well, looks like this year is off. Good thing my passport is good for a few years. I'll just plan to go next year."

The next day was Dad's last radiation treatment for his neck area. While we were very excited to be done with this four week journey, we were apprehensive about what course of treatment Dr. Go and team would prescribe for this new issue.

After a series of consultations, they determined that the best option would be another four weeks of radiation this type focused on the groin area. As family members, we were skeptical about more treatments, however Dad viewed this as just another bump in the road and agreed to begin the treatments the very next day.

Dad remained mentally positive; but was growing physically very weak. My husband and I would meet him every day at the clinic for his radiation treatment and were able to tell how he was feeling just by the way he walked. We would typically arrive a few minutes earlier than Dad watching him pull into the parking spots specifically designated for radiation patients. Some days he would get out of his pickup truck quickly and arrive in the lobby in his usual bubbly manner; other days his gate was slow and labored. What never changed however was his positive attitude. He remained steadfast in his resolve and determination to beat cancer.

One day we arrived at the clinic at our usual time only to find Dad already in the lobby. We commented that we had not seen his pick-up in the parking lot. He smiled and proudly proclaimed that he had purchased a new pickup truck. We were very surprised by this as his previous truck was not that old. He explained that he had never really liked the color of the previous truck (again another example of a marriage compromise). It was white...he wanted a red one. So, in typical fashion, he had traded in the white one for a brand new red pickup truck complete with topper. He was very proud of the fact that he did this without any permission from anyone, especially permission from us kids.

Throughout this entire process he never missed a day of driving bus. He loved his kids and they loved him back. The kids noticed his weight loss and kept expressing their concern. One mother jumped on the bus when Dad was dropping off her kids and asked if there was something that Dad was hungry for. He quickly replied, "Baked chicken and potatoes". This was at approximate 3 pm. That same day at roughly 5 pm, the family showed up at the house with baked chicken, mashed potatoes and of course corn. They even brought a homemade banana cream pie.

This type of outpouring was typical. For many of the Bus Number 7 kids, this was the first time that someone they knew and saw every day was experiencing cancer. They were doing whatever they could think of to make things better. Cards, pictures, food, and even a promise of good behavior from several of his troublemakers.

One of his little girls who was quite shy had read in the church bulletin that Richard's cancer had returned. During the service she drew a card and wrote in the card that she needed him to get better. She ran up the isle to find him after the service and handed it to him along with a big hug. Dad was overwhelmed.

The weeks that followed were difficult. The realization of Mom's death coupled with Dad's recent diagnosis were taking a toll. Dad was having difficulty climbing the stairs. Their two story house did not have a bedroom or shower on the first floor. Mom and Dad had talked multiple times about remodeling to add a bedroom and full bath to the first floor. Dad had even roughed up the plans in accordance with Mom's ideas.

With Dad's significant decline in strength and our commitment to not put him into a nursing home, we decided it was time to remodel and put that bedroom and full bath on the main floor. Dad was super excited by this idea. He went into his shop and before we knew it he produced a rough sketch of the design.

It was the perfect solution to meet Dad's needs with minimal work to the exterior of the house although quite major adjustments to the interior first floor. Word spread quickly about the remodeling project. When people found out what needed to be done, they eagerly offered their services, mostly free of charge. The saying "many hands make light work" was certainly appropriate in this case. His Bus Number 7 kids, past and present, once again came through offering skills and materials to help complete the job. Work started on the remodel project the last weekend in October and was complete by Christmas.

Dad actively participated in all phases of this project picking out carpet, paint and overseeing the "construction" volunteers. Despite being extremely weak, he also decided to make himself a bed (headboard, footboard and attached drawers under the bed). He had two purposes in mind, or at least this is what he said. He could make the bed the exact height to accommodate little or no effort in getting into and/or out of bed and he would use the drawers for storage as there was limited space in his bedroom for a another piece of furniture. With only an idea in his head, he created a beautiful oak bed that is still used by his great grandson Grayson to this day.

Halloween was always special for Dad's Bus Number 7 kids. Since his kids all lived in the country, Halloween was a time for them to be able to come to town and go trick or treating. Dad loved to dress up and Mom always made sure they had plenty of candy so as to give his Bus Number 7 kids extra treats. They both made sure that there were pumpkins on the porch and "scary" decorations welcoming the little ones.

Even though this was the first year without Mom, Dad was doing his best to make sure this tradition carried on. He bought special treats and made plans to wear his "chemo mask". At the last minute however he decided that the mask was a little too intense especially for his younger kids so opted for a scarecrow face. He was surprised to return from his bus route one evening to see that "someone" had left pumpkins on the front porch and had decorated the front steps. Although Dad never found out who did this, he knew that his Bus Number 7 kids and parents were behind the kind gesture. They realized Dad had not put up decorations and thought this would help put him in the holiday spirit.

By the way decorations "magically" appeared as Christmas approached complete with a lit holiday wreath on their front door. Dad was humbled by their kindness.

Heart Issue

In addition to cancer Dad also had an aneurism on his aorta. He always said that he was more worried about this than the cancer. It had now grown to the point where surgery was needed. The preliminary workup showed that Dad was not a candidate for the surgery because of the location of the aneurism. The repair would involve open invasive surgery. Given Dad's weakened physical state the cardiovascular surgeon felt that this type of surgery would require a recovery that would be too much for him.

The Doctor explained the situation to my father. Dad sat there for a while and then asked the doctor to diagram the situation for him. He did what Dad had asked for and then proceeded to show him again why the non-invasive procedure was not an option. Dad shook his head and sat quietly as the Doctor began to dictate his case notes. Once he was done Dad said, "Now I realize that I really don't know anything about this but why couldn't you bypass one of my kidneys and repair the aneurism using the noninvasive process?" Dad went on to say said he was certain that he could live without one kidney. The Doctor looked puzzled but agreed to discuss the matter with a general surgeon.

A couple of days later the phone rang. It was Dad's cardiologist. Sure enough Dad's idea would work. If Dad was willing, they would do the procedure over Christmas vacation. Dad thought was this was great; he would not need to miss any school or worry his kids. Despite Dad needing blood transfusions due to low blood counts resulting from the chemo, he came through the surgery with flying colors. After an overnight hospital stay he was back on his feet. Dad took a drawing of the procedure with to his coffee buddies explaining exactly what had taken place. They were very impressed.

His bus kids heard about his holiday surgery and were eager to ask him questions about this. Dad told them that they should always look for other ways of doing things and to never settle for what other people might tell you until you are satisfied with the answer. Dad used this experience as a life lesson for his kids. Even though my father did not have a formal education beyond his high school degree he certainly was an intelligent man.

Cancer Tightens Its Grip

The extended Christmas holiday gave Dad some extra time to regain his strength. He was eating relatively well and was excited to be still able to take his fair share of special extra-curricular bus outings. Three days before New Year's Eve, he had agreed to drive the Westby wrestling team to La Crosse for regional tournaments. He was to have the team in La Crosse at the convention center by 7 am and return them to Westby that night around midnight. The weather was terribly cold so we convinced Dad to stay at our house with his bus parked out front until it was time to go pick up the kids. This allowed him to warm up the bus every couple of hours and take a nap prior to going to the convention center at 11:30 pm. Dad was in especially good spirits that day. He was very proud to still be "carrying his weight" as a bus driver. We took him for a special dinner at a local restaurant, Schmidty's, where he enjoyed his favorite, shrimp scampi. When we returned he promptly fell asleep for a three hour nap. Good thing my husband had set an alarm. He woke in time to warm the bus, have a cup of hot chocolate and pick up his kids.

The day of his final radiation treatment was once again here. With great anticipation we visited the radiologist who had loosely promised to eradicate Dad's cancer to review the latest scans. Just as he brought up the scan on the monitor, we noticed a disturbing look on his face. Damn cancer he said. Lymphoma had now taken the upper hand. Just when we thought we were ahead of the lymphoma another area would surface. This time there were new tumors in the stomach area. Despite his previous, we can beat this demeanor, this time he was soft spoken and contrite. He said the best thing we could do was to go back to Dr. Go, Dad's oncologist for possible options.

We scheduled an appointment with Dr. Go for the next day. Dr. Go's entire extended team, all who knew us very well at this point, gathered that morning in the tiny examination room to discuss potential options. Unfortunately Dad had tried everything that was medically available. His weight had now dropped to 140 pounds. At this point we were out of options. We spent over an hour talking through Dad's situation. Finally Dr. Go, with tears in his eyes and a crack in his voice, said that there was nothing more to be done. He immediately hugged Dad and suggested that we sign up for hospice and begin palliative care.

Sitting next to my Dad, I felt his disappointment and knew the stark reality ahead. He sat there for a few minutes and then in a very slow and deliberate manner said this probably meant it was time to hang up his Bus Number 7 keys. With these few words, the entire room began to cry. This team of medical professionals had been with Dad through not only his health issues but through Mom's death. They cared deeply and knew that Dad's time was running out. Dad did his best to console and calm the group. He said, "Hey you guys know me. No pity party here. We just need to focus now and deal with the situation at hand". That was it, we packed up our things, took the hospice information and left the clinic.

Time to Hang Up Bus Number 7 Keys

He returned to Westby and immediately talked with his supervisor about his prognosis and decision to hang up his Bus Number 7 key. This was a very tough day for Dad. Short and to the point, he told his supervisor the news and left his key at the garage. When his supervisor told him he still had over 80 days of sick time, he merely shrugged his shoulders and suggested he give them to someone who tends to get sick!

He then drove the short distance to their church where he spent time with Pastor Julie. He asked for prayers and blessings to get through the next few months. Word travelled fast in their little with an outpouring of support and acts of kindness from the community.

One of the first things Dad asked me to help him with was to assist in writing a letter to "his kids". He felt compelled to write a letter to the kids on his bus explaining to them what had happened and to share with them what he found so special about each one and every one of them.

This project took several days to accomplish. I would type as Dad dictated to me. As weak as Dad was, I was amazed at how methodically he went through his route. He started with the first stop of the morning and filed through every single stop. He took time to reminisce about each one and was disappointed when he would say someone's name and not have a lot to say about them. Some of the kids only rode periodically being transported to school instead by one of their parents. His disappointment was in the fact that he had not gotten to know them well enough to really give any comment. Below is a copy of the letter that was mailed to each of "his kids".

January 18, 2008

> *Dear Family and Friends of Bus Number 7,*
>
> *This past week I learned that my illness has progressed to the point where I will no longer be able to drive bus. You are ALL so important to me. Whether you've only ridden one year or for many years we have*

grown to become the "Family of Bus Number 7". Each one of you has touched my heart in a special way. I am writing this letter to you to let you what I most remember about each of you.

My first pickup of the morning, the Korn family. To Sam, Sadie and Garrison- What a wonderful site to come over the hill and see you guys jumping up and down hoping it is me driving the bus. I honk several times to let you know it is in fact me and I see you all get even more excited. Your excitement made my day. It is something I will never forget! To Mom Korn – thank you for the hugs and all the fresh, (always warm) cookies and treats. I don't know how you did it. Your children are very lucky to have such a wonderful mom. To Garrison- I know how much you wanted me to drive again next year. I am sorry that I will not be able to do that; but just know how much I will be thinking about you.

To Karly and Lucas-Lucas, well you always had a bit of the devil in you- but in a good way. You are going to be a fine young man someday. Karly, your smile is infectious. It is enough to melt a person. I'm sure that your Mom would agree. To Mom Anderson-Your waves from the door when I dropped the kids off will always be remembered.

To the Leum kids. To Lexi –You were always so cheerful and bubbly. I especially enjoyed how you took care of your brothers. To Brock – How many times you told me how nice it was to see me back driving. You were always cheerful; although you and Sam would get into it once and a while; which for me was no big deal. To Bjorn – What a guy! You liked to have fun. There were things that happened on the bus that we just let stay on the bus. Kind of like Las Vegas – What happens there stays there. Between you and Gunnar Hanson "pretend shooting", there really shouldn't have been any deer, birds, etc., left on our route. Remember I told you the problem was you guys never did hit anything. To Mom Leum- Thank you for being the "secret" decorator! The pumpkins for Halloween and the Christmas wreath for the holiday were great. Little did you know that I would find out it was you guys. Thank you so much.

To the Stebins girls-It was always nice to see your shiny faces in the morning; even though some mornings I would drive in but end up with no riders. Wish I could have waited around; but you know how it is...

To the Sherry children – I wish it would have been more than just two times a week that you guys rode the bus. What a joy to have you guys running out to the bus always greeting me with a big hello. No matter where I was, at church or any place else you guys would always come up to me and give me a high five. By the way I got the cool picture and note you made during church. Thank you!

To the Bakkums' – Congratulations, your family is my third generation family. That's right, I have driven long enough to have three generations of Bakkum's. No matter what Bakkum's I have had in all these years; Bakkums are Bakkums and they are all great! Thank goodness none of you kids turned out like your Uncle Curt Bakkum (just kidding). He was and still is one of my best friends. So please look up to your uncle.

To the Spiller's-Although I did not get to know you that well since you only started riding my bus this year you were very special to me because you always, always had a smile. You would just make my day. I wish I would have known you longer.

To Cody Meyer – There you would be sound asleep when we would get to school in the morning. I hope you keep on having good naps and that there is always someone on the bus to wake you up.

To Lars and Makayla – So memorable were your smiles, warm hellos and wonderful treats. Lars, I'm glad we got your schedule figured out so that we would know if you were going home or to your Grandpa's. To Mom Gretebeck -thank you for all the concern, the hugs and the wonderful dinner you brought to the house. I will never forget your friendly waves. What a good feeling it was to know that you trusted me with your kids.

To Taylor Anderson – I will always remember how very quiet you were. My goal was to get you to say good morning and good by before I was no longer driving. Guess I didn't quite get there but perhaps you will consider that for the driver who replaces me. A hello or hi goes a long way. Good luck to you.

To Cody and Riley See – Unfortunately, I did not get to know you very well in the short time that you rode my bus; but to Riley – good luck wresting. I know you will make your folks proud. Cody you have a nice smile. Somehow I always thought you were a Bakkum, (which from what I said earlier was a good thing); best of everything to you.

To Kinza Eiserman – you were always on time no matter what time I came. You are a very nice quiet girl who was never any trouble. You were someone who seemed to enjoy going to school. May you continue to enjoy your education.

To Shelby Gagermeier – My little mother hen. You don't know how many times you helped me by helping get kids ready to get off the bus. If there was a problem you were always there. You are one of those kids who loved to help others. You have such a big heart Shelby and certainly hold a big place in my heart.

To Tyler Icke – It would have been really fun to have actually talked with you; without your headset and iPod. Just a quick hi or bye now and again would have been great. Good luck in future years.

To Logan Bjerkos – What a honey! You always wanted to know what was going on with my health. Your mom told me that when she told you I had cancer you said, "how come my two favorite people have cancer?" Logan although not always easy to understand, just trust that God has a plan for each of us. Thank you for the warm sweatshirt and for t "our secret wave and honk" once I knew that you were safe in your house. Always a smile; always a good morning; and always a good by. I am sure you will make your parents proud!

To Hilary Grim – My, oh my, how you have grown up in the years you have ridden my bus. You have gone from a puny little girl to a beautiful young lady. Oh what a change this has been! It has been my privilege to have known you. You will go a long way Hillary – keep up the good work.

To Gunnar, Sam and Zach – To Gunnar – We certainly had a challenge getting you to actually "sit" on the seat (which of course is what they are for) and for you and Bjorn to stop "shooting" everything in sight. Once we got those two items under control you have been a super guy. By the way, I think you must have been shooting blanks since you guys were never hit anything!?

To Zach and Sam – Treat your step dad with respect because some day you may be as prominent as him!!!!!!!! Good luck in whatever you pursue. You are two well-liked young men.

To Erica Holen – Always, always, always a "Good morning Richard". I always enjoyed those little secrets you would slide up and tell me. Never a dull moment! What a sweetheart! Your Mom and Dad should be proud.

To Katlyn – I regret not getting to know you better. From what I have observed, you are going to be a very outstanding young lady.

To Hunter – What can I say!? We certainly had our ups and downs. I am sure there were times when you thought I was the worst person around. Then before I knew it, you would turn around and tell me how much you loved me. Oh, how you warmed my heart. One of my goals this year was to make sure you and Lucas liked each other. Hunter let me give you this advice, before you blow up the next time, count to ten and think about one good thing in this world you would like to have happen. If you do this you may be surprised that you may no longer be upset.

To Hunter's parents – I wanted everything to be right between the boys. In fact at the time I left driving I thought things were going quite well. My wish is that this can continue.

To Hunter's Grandpa and Grandma – I am glad that we had our talks and that we both understood what Hunter was going through as well as what I was going through. It was a good feeling knowing you were supporting me. Best of luck to you.

To Emma and Grace – You are the nicest girls!! You have been my shining light ever since you moved to the valley and rode on my bus. When I got sick you were both so concerned and would always ask how I was doing. I am proud of you both for all your accomplishments – Snow queen and Syttende Mai queen. I am sure your parents are very proud of you. To Dad Homstad – When I took the kids to the Twin Cities to go to Costa Rica you opened your home to the kids and my wife. This was absolutely unreal and a great experience. Thank you. To Mom Homstad – The last time we talked I thought you were one of the kids waiting to get on the bus. I put my red lights on, opened the door, only to have you come on and give me a hug that never seemed to quit. You told me to take good care of myself. I will never forget it.

To Arielle – Always there--You and your Grandpa. You always wanted to know what time I would be home so that you could call Grandpa. What a responsible young lady.

To Herman and Hillary Feller- Oh Hillary, what a fine young lady you have grown up to be. I've seen you go from a spindly little girl to a lovely young lady. A lot like MOM!!!!! Good luck in whatever you do. To Herman – Remember those times when you were sleeping and I drove by your house – sorry about that. I would see your hand come up and knew we had to turn around. You never seemed to mind just a smile and a laugh. I hear what a great basketball player you are. I always wanted to see you make first string varsity on the Westby basketball team; I never got to see you play. Good luck to you as well.

To Justen Aarness – Although you have not ridden this year, I have certainly missed you and wish you the best in the future.

To Devin Hansen – Thank God that water puddle in front of your house was not any deeper as it would have gone over your shoes. If there was a puddle you found it. Even though your mother would tell you to stay of the puddle; you keep on trucking paying no attention to your Mom. On the other hand, you always did look at me before you crossed in front of the bus. I was proud of you for that. You will grow up to be a fine young man someday.

To Dillen and Caycee Bean – Such predictable conscientious young kids. Your conduct was such that it was always a pleasure to have you both on my bus. You were always there – never any trouble. I appreciated that!

To Lexi and Trey – Although you did not "officially" ride my bus, we somehow became fast friends. I remember you both being so excited to see me and giving me big hugs at the beginning of the school year because I was back driving. Trey, I'll never forget your words of comfort after my wife passed away. You told me how very sorry you were for my loss. You are both very caring compassionate people. I wish you could have ridden my bus!

Fifty three years ago, I started to drive school bus so that my family would have health insurance. We were dairy farming at the time, so money was not abundant. As the years went on however, I realized how much I really enjoyed driving. In fact at the end of my bus driving career, it was you, my bus families that really brought sunshine to my days. The day I had to "hang up my bus key" was one of the toughest days of my life. To all my bus families, I'd like to thank you for all you have given me especially the privilege of spending time with your children. And so with that I say farewell for now...my thoughts and prayers will be with you always!

With this project behind him, Dad tried his best to not dwell on his situation. He would try to go to morning coffee with his buddies and would visit with friends in the afternoon to help pass time. He would check in on the kitchen floor project at the church. The money from Mom's memorial was going to good use replacing the concrete uneven floors in the basement kitchen. He knew she would be pleased that some of the money was going for this purpose. One day when Dad was in the church kitchen checking on progress, he noticed that there were heavy overhead doors that had to be opened in order to serve the dining room from the kitchen. He watched the women in the kitchen struggle to open these and decided he should make new doors. He would make doors that would slide from side to side and not need to be fastened overhead.

This project would keep him in his woodworking shop for numerous hours. The project involved fourteen doors. As the weeks wore on and he became weaker, we realized that he was probably not going to be able to finish all of them. One evening after we had dinner with Dad he said, "Hey Toots, if you can help me get into my shop clothes I'll take you into my shop and show you how to make a door". Much to my surprise that is just what we did. Dad gave me instructions and gently guided me through the process. There I was with my safety goggles protecting my eyes, clothes covered in sawdust running a table saw for the first time in my life. Unfortunately that was the last time he was able to get to his shop. He became too weak to operate any equipment and said he couldn't find the energy to keep teaching me. He told me to wash up his shop clothes and give them to the needy. His days in the shop he said were behind him.

The bus kids and families that received Dad's letter were very touched. For many of the kids, it was the first time they had seen their name in such a formal looking document. Parents found themselves consoling and counseling their kids as for many this was also the first time they were losing a person they knew so well. One little boy sent a card and a note that said the substitute driver didn't know what he was doing and couldn't he please come back and drive the bus.

During this time Dad had many, many visitors. In addition to family and friends, many of his bus families, past and present stopped by the house to spend time with Dad. They took turns bringing food to the house so that Dad or the immediate family member would not have to worry about food preparation. Sitting there with Dad during many of these conversations was very special. I couldn't help but captured several of the stories that seemed to bring the biggest laughter or largest nods of satisfaction and fulfillment. Several of my favorites are as follows:

The imaginary dog

My father took his driving responsibilities very seriously. He was a strict driver not allowing the kids to get away with too much mischief. The youngest of his riders sitting right behind him just like little ducks behind the mother duck or in this case the father duck. He said he did this not only for safety purposes but also to make sure the older kids were not picking on any of the little ones.

He also had a great sense of humor and had a very special way of making his point when necessary. He would occasionally have kids, especially boys, who could just not sit still. He would explain to them the importance of sitting (not standing) while the bus was moving and also warned them of the safety issue caused by moving around from seat to seat They could potentially cause harm not only to themselves but to others as well. Regardless of how many times Dad warned them, they continued to move about freely on his bus.

One day, while first making sure no cars or any hazards were in his way, he slammed on the brakes. He set up the air brakes causing the bus to suddenly come to a stop. "A dog", my Dad exclaimed. "A dog coming out of nowhere suddenly crossing the road", he expressed in a convincing voice. Both boys were caught off guard. First of all they knew they should have been sitting in their seats and secondly they were scared beyond words. One of the boys slid along the center isle ending up right next to my Dad's seat. Its ok, it's ok the little boy quickly cried out. He was obviously shaken but not about to let on to Dad. Both boys quickly got up and returned to their seats promising from that day on to always stay seated while the bus was moving. Both boys had learned a very valuable lesson.

As Dad listened to this story he started to laugh hysterically. There had been no dog, he had made up the entire deal. Dad went on to explain that he had used this technique throughout the years whenever he had kids that were not heading his warnings. An interesting way to make his point; but one that certain accomplished his goal.

Teaching moments- boys not getting along

Dad much like the Vegas advertisement had the philosophy of what happens on the bus stays on the bus. One year quite late in Dad's bus driving career, he encountered two second grade boys who really disliked each other. This dislike occurred not only on the bus but also in the class room. The boys' teacher approached Dad to ask for his help to get the boys to work through their differences. Dad reluctantly agreed to use the approach the teacher suggested however he soon became very frustrated with her approach. She had decided the best way to handle this was to separate the boys and provide a written summary to the parents at the end of each day as to any incidents or behaviors that she noticed that were disturbing.

This went on for several weeks with no improvement in behavior. It was obvious to Dad that the parents either had no control over their kids or did not really care.

It was then that Dad decided that a more direct approach was in order. Rather than have the two boys sit at opposite ends of the bus, he required that they share a sit, sitting directly behind him for the first week. He was appalled to hear the language and witness the physical confrontations between the two boys.

One morning as they arrived at school, he asked the two of them to stay behind for a little chat. It was then that Dad told them if he ever heard them use foul language again he would make sure there would be consequences. What the boys did not realize is that my father knew each of the boy's grandfather's. Dad shared this with the boys and explained that if their behavior persisted he would get their grandfather's involved. The boys' eyes immediately widened. It was obvious that neither of the boy's wanted to have their grandparents know of their behavior. From that day one, there was a marked improvement in their behavior. In fact they turned out to be good friends. The teacher stopped by the bus several days later and asked if Dad knew what caused the boys to change. Dad merely explained, "What happens on the bus, stays on the bus". This became a favorite mantra for Dad as the years passed.

Drive slow today or I might get sick

One day as Dad waited in the bus line for school to dismiss, one of his youngest riders, a little kindergarten girl came running out of school and up the steps onto Dad's bus. She stopped, moved as close as she could get to Dad and whispered into his ear. "Richard, I am not feeling good so if you do not want me to throw up on your bus, please drive slow today." Needless to say, Dad took her seriously and drove as slowly. He even gave her a "barf bag" and had her sit directly behind him as the farther you get to the back of the bus, the bumpier the ride.

His efforts however were for enough. About half way through his route, just as he started down the driveway to the girl's home, she tapped Dad on the shoulder, leaned forward and threw up all over Dad and the bus. Good thing Dad had a strong stomach and had endured a lot distasteful things during his time as a father and farmer. He quickly grabbed some wipes (Mom insisted he keep some on his bus for emergencies), stopped the bus and consoled the little girl. He had the kids wait on the bus while he walked her to the front door and waited for the mother to answer. After a quick explanation he was back on the bus to continue his route. He had stripped down to just his undershirt, packing his soiled flannel shirt in a plastic bag.

The story of what happened that day was quick to circulate among the other drivers and family members of Dad's riders. Since Dad was known for being a "quick," rather aggressive driver, they would often tease him if he did not slow down, they were going to get sick.

Forgetting to drop off a little girl during the evening route

As previously mentioned, Dad took his responsibility as a bus driver very seriously so imagine his shock when he realized that one of his first graders had fallen asleep on the bus on the way home from school. This was a little girl who rode periodically so Dad did not think it unusual when he did not see her through his rear view mirror as he neared her home. He drove the entire route and returned to the bus garage just like a normal day. As he was doing his end of the day walk through of the bus he noticed the little one sound asleep in the last seat of the bus. He immediately woke her, assured her everything was fine and then phoned the girl's mother to let her know what had happened and promised to have her delivered home within the next 30 minutes. The little girl, now sitting directly behind Dad received a solo ride to her home. She thought the attention was great, chatting the entire ride home. Thank goodness the mother was also in good spirits when Dad delivered the little girl to her doorstep

Girlfriend

The school busses line up just in time for the release of the kids in the afternoon. Dad parked right behind a younger driver, Stan with whom several years earlier Dad had befriended. He was a younger farmer who truly loved my Dad. His father had died at a young age and Dad provided the much needed father touch. He talked with him daily and was always there to give advice.

Dad also had a couple of teacher friends who would come and talk to him at the end of the Day. Dad loved the attention. One of the teachers, Lori, was a close personal friend. When Lori was on bus patrol duty, she would make a point of coming on Dad's bus and giving him a big hug and a kiss on the cheek. This would always bring the kids on the bus to a standing round of cheers. They would say that "Richard had a girlfriend" over and over again. Stan could hear the commotion and started to wander if this could actually be true. How would he break the news to Ilene? Dad enjoyed every minute of this folly that continued for almost the entire school year. Lori also found it entertaining playing along to add to the drama.

Recognized from the back of his head

For my father's 70th birthday, my husband and I took Mom and Dad to a very nice restaurant in downtown La Crosse for dinner. We enjoyed a delicious meal and were about to order dessert (my father loved dessert) when a young waiter approached the table. He said with a big smile, "Hi Richard. Do you remember me?" Dad, looking a bit puzzled admitted that he did not recognize the young lad. The young man quickly replied with his name followed by, "You were my bus driver for twelve years. I graduated ten years ago and am now assistant chef at this restaurant". The minute the young man said his name Dad remembered him. They immediately embraced and began a lively half hour chat about old times. As we were leaving, Dad asked the young man how he had recognized Dad after so many years. He quickly responded, "From the back of your head". After so many years of staring at you from the back of the bus, I would never forget that head and bald spot". Dad got a real kick out of that!

Class trip to Mexico

It was customary for the senior class to take a class trip at the end of the school year. One year, late in Dad's driving career the class was going to Mexico and needed a bus driver to transport them to and from the Minneapolis airport (roughly 3 ½ hours from Westby). This meant two round trips for Dad as the kids were going to be gone for roughly a week.

Dad agreed to take this trip knowing that most of the drivers would avoid taking trip. Most were not comfortable driving bus outside the Westby community. He proudly announced to his fellow bus drivers that he would be happy to take this extra-curricular trip citing his numerous prior trip to places such as Madison and Chicago. When he shared the news with Mom however she was not so thrilled. Dad had just finished an aggressive round of chemo and she was worried about his ability to drive that distance without becoming exhausted. As a compromise he agreed to stop for breaks (once he had dropped the kids off) and take along a cell phone so that Mom could reach him if needed. Note this was at a time before cell phones were real common. The bus had a CB radio however there was no way for mom to be in touch.

The drop off round trip was uneventful. The kids were accompanied by several chaperones and their teacher. The teacher had taken students on trips such as this in the past however for most of the kids and chaperones this was their first big trip involving airfare and a major airport.

The challenge occurred during the return leg of the trip. Pickup time was set for 10 pm assuming the flight was on time. By the way Mom was even more upset when she learned the late pick up time. This meant that at the earliest Dad would be back home was around 2 am. With Mom's coaching Dad decided to drive to a truck stop roughly 25 minutes from the Minneapolis airport late in the day. This way he could have dinner there, take a nap in the bus and then drive the short distance for the pickup around 9:15 pm. Mom was to call him around this time in case his wrist alarm did not wake him. This sounded like a great plan. The only problem was Dad accidently turned off the cell phone and slept through his alarm. Mom tried many times to call but to no avail. By 10 pm the school was calling Mom at home. Dad had not shown up at the airport. The bus supervisor was not able to reach Dad via the CB. Everyone was starting to panic. Mom remembered that my husband and I were in Minneapolis staying at a hotel. She called us telling of the situation. We got into our car and drove to the bus stop only to find Dad fast asleep. He had laid down in one of the seats and dozed off. He was mortified to learn that he was late. He quickly assembled himself and drove to the airport. This time he was met with not such a happy crowd. By now they had been waiting for roughly an hour with their luggage sitting outside the airport. Although happy to see him and glad he was fine, they were tired and eager to get home. Roughly three hours later he pulled into the school parking lot where all the parents and family members had been waiting for the pickup. Most were in very good spirits giving Dad a bad time for what had happened.

Good thing Dad had a good sense of humor. Needless to say the next Monday at the bus garage his fellow drivers gave him a hard time. Dad just shrugged, laughed and said, "Well it could have been worse. I might have been dead. Then one of you would have had to drive to Minneapolis." Nothing more was said.

Time to Celebrate Richard

Finally the day arrived when Dad reluctantly realized that it was time to move forward with the hospice paperwork. As hospice volunteers, my husband and I realized that it was beneficial to get setup for this service sooner versus later. We encouraged Dad to at least complete the paperwork and go through the initial assessment. The assessment showed that Dad was in pretty good shape and at this point would only need to be seen only once a week. Despite missing his bus routine and kids he was doing quite well.

It was roughly a week later when then the doors fell off the bus, so to speak. He was struggling for breadth and was very uncomfortable. His lungs had filled with fluid and he had severe pain in his abdomen. This was the first and only time Dad ever complained about his situation. I was helping him get out of bed in the morning when he said, "If this is how it is going to be and I am going to feel like this it is certainly no way to live." It was then that we knew the end was relatively near. Hospice nurses started to come on a daily basis. Within a week the hospice nurses determined that he was "actively dying". This term I had not previously heard of and one that I found very odd and disturbing. They conducted a series of tests and concluded that Dad's body was shutting down.

Word of Dad's quick decline brought about an idea from several of his current "Bus Number 7 mother's". They wanted to have a celebration party for Dad. Late one day two of them came to the house to talk about their plan. They wanted to have a get together with Dad and his bus kids at the school cafeteria to share memories and celebrate Dad's life. Dad loved the idea. We picked a date that accommodated everyone's busy schedules. The party would be three weeks from now. A week before the date, Dad's condition further declined. I called the organizers to tell them we did not think Dad would be able to attend the party as he was very weak. They said they wanted to keep the date even though he may not be able to come in person.

We learned that the number of people planning to attend Dad's party was continuing to grow. Word of mouth about the event spread quickly with families from previous years, going all the way back to the late 50's were planning to attend. The guest list was expanding to include not only current bus kids and family but also previous riders.

Dad's condition continued to worsen but he remained determined that he was going to attend this event. He had me purchase small gold cross with a flying dove lapel pins as a token gift for him to give to each of his current bus kids. He wanted to personally give this to the kids the day of the party. We made arrangements with the mothers who were hosting the party to have Dad meet with his current kids in a special room for the presentation and pictures. Dad was super excited to have some alone time with his current crew.

The day of the party finally arrived. Dad was extremely weak but was determined none the less to attend. By now Dad was on oxygen and was using a walker or wheel chair to get around. He told me however the there was no way he was going to miss this event. His kids wanted to honor him and thank him for his years of service. He wanted to celebrate with them, let them know everything would be ok and to tell them to not worry about him. He wanted to physically look good so we took great care in picking out a bright red shirt and khaki pants. He told me Mom would have wanted him to look bright and chipper. We chuckled at his comment but agreed that this would have been her wish. We helped him into the car and drove the short four block distance to the high school cafeteria where the party was being held. As we came around the corner we were totally surprised by the number of cars and people at the party. We parked the car right outside the entrance and were immediately welcomed by several of his prior bus kids now in their late 50's. He managed to use his walker to enter the party feeling quite proud that he had enough strength to stand on his own.

He met with his current bus kids and gave each one his little gift. We then gathered everyone together for pictures with Dad seated front and center.

The kids seemed rather subdued probably because they were unsure what to say in a situation such as this. One thing was clear however, they all wanted to stand as close to my Dad as they could. As they huddled together one of the older boys began telling Dad how slow and "bad" the substitute driver was. The rest of the kids were quick to chime in and add to the comments. They were clearly not happy with Dad's substitute many asking if and when Dad would be back. Dad just smiled and shrugged his shoulders. Several of the little ones had made pictures and were pushing in line to try and get Dad's attention with their special art piece. The mothers had also put together a scrapbook of current riders. Dad was very touched by their sentiments.

It was now time for Dad and his current kids to join the rest of the people at the party. As Dad entered the general cafeteria area, he was greeted by several rousing rounds of "for he is a jolly good fellow". Dad was clearly overwhelmed with the number of people that were there. The high school cafeteria was packed. Dad beamed as he was presented with an award for his years of service and a large cake decorated with a yellow Bus Number 7. Everyone cheered as he thanked them for coming and encouraged them to get a piece of cake before he ate it all. His sense of humor was still intact. The rest of the afternoon was spent reminiscing about the years spent on Dad's bus, sharing old pictures and posing with Dad for pictures. There was what seemed to be an endless line of people vying for Dad's attention. One family had three generations at the party. Their stories and pictures told it all. Dad, despite not initially wanting to drive school bus ended up being a fixture in the community influencing the lives of many over his 50+ years of driving. Even Dad's the little blond trouble maker came to the party. He was as you might expect no longer blonde instead being quite bald, just like Dad. It was obvious to most, he was still a favorite of Dad's. Laughter filled the cafeteria; clearly everyone was having a great time.

Dad posing with the kids that were on his bus that year Grades

Approximately two hours after arriving at the cafeteria, Dad pulled me close to him and whispered that it was time for him to go. He was visibly tired and was much more pale than he had been just hours ago. As we prepared to leave the cafeteria, his kids continued to vie for his attention. They stayed as close to his wheel chair as they could. Just as we reached the doorway several of his younger kids started to chant, "Go Richard go, go Richard go, go Richard go!" Soon everyone in the room was chanting. Dad closed his eyes and gave a gentle wave as we left the building. Helping him into the car, I reached across to secure his seat belt. He gently grabbed my arm and said, "Hey Toots, quite the party huh? Now it's time to go home.

While this may seem hard believe, during the four block drive from the school cafeteria to Mom and Dad's house, Dad fell into a deep sleep. We managed to wake him just long enough to get him into the house, into some comfortable clothes and situated in his favorite leather recliner. No further words were said. That evening he slipped into a coma. He never regained consciousness. It seemed as though he had been living to see "his kids" one more time. By the end of his fifty-three years of he had grown to love driving Bus Number 7 now viewing every minute of every trip a privilege.

While we had hospice in place and thought we were prepared to have Dad pass away at home, this was not to be. Despite being in a coma, he seemed restless and uncomfortable. We decided to call the ambulance and have him taken to La Crosse Lutheran Hospital. As the ambulance arrived, the young neighbor boy who years earlier Dad had saved from the bats watched and waved as Dad left the house on a stretcher. "Thanks Richard…you are the best", the young man said. The young gentleman from the ambulance service also a prior bus kid waved back, smiled and told the neighbor kid he couldn't agree more. Thankfully they allowed me to ride in the back of the ambulance with Dad for the 30 mile drive to the hospital.

Three days later Dad passed away.

The day of the funeral the weather was a dreadful mix of snow, rain and sleet. The school administration had made the decision to call off school that day because of the weather. This was something Dad typically scoffed at, saying that the drivers were professionals and were certainly capable of handling tough weather; fully understanding that student safety was always the top priority. Today, however I think Dad would have felt differently. He would have been extremely pleased that his kids and fellow drivers would be able to attend his funeral without the consequence of missing school.

The service was just as Dad would have liked complete with inspirational words, songs sung by his granddaughters, instrumental music provided by a fellow bus driver and of course vocal selections by long-time friend Fritz accompanied on the organ by Mrs. Nelson. Unaware that the weather continued to get worse as the service proceeded, we were surprised to see the mortician quietly hand the Pastor a note just as the service was about to conclude. Just prior to the processional, he announced that due to the extremely slippery road conditions they were asking that only the immediate family attend the graveside service. There had been talk of a bus procession, but weather was not going to permit that.

The rest of the congregation was asked to go immediately to the church basement for refreshments and fellowship. Funny, but I felt Dad's hand at work. He would not have wanted his bus kids, young and or old see his body lowered into the ground.

When we arrived back at the church, the warmth, aroma of coffee and the sounds of young voices and people laughing filled the church. The fellowship hall was overflowing with groups of people reminiscing about their bus days with Dad. It was obvious Dad's spirit was alive and well. Just as Dad's kids had touched his life so profoundly, it was obvious that he too had profoundly impacted each of their lives and would live on in their hearts for years to come.

Epilogue

The days, months and years since Mom and Dad's death have been challenging. Losing both parents in such a short period of time was unsettling at first but as time passes I have come to realize that this was just as Mom and Dad would have wanted it. They loved life and lived it to the fullest. One would not have done well without the other. I also think having lost Mom to sudden death and Dad to a prolonged illness taught those of us left behind a great deal. Life is short, be sure to tell those you love how much they mean…you never know when your last day may be.

As I reflected on those final days with Dad I wrote him a tribute. It helped me to come to terms with his passing.

Tribute to my Dad

"Hey Toots…I'm having a good day today!" Just two weeks ago, those were the words I heard as you answered the phone from your woodworking shop. That was you, always a positive can-do attitude. You were such a positive role-model to so many people.

What I remember most about you was how hard you worked. I know that in the early years of farming, with a wife and three young children to provide for, money was very tight. In addition to farming you were driving bus, raising tobacco and doing roofing jobs on the side just to stay ahead. What an incredible work ethic! Even when times were really tough, like when the barn burned, or the tornado destroyed the tobacco shed and silo you and Mom would just put your heads together and figure out a way to continue on. I do not EVER recall you complaining. You just did what you had to do to provide for your family.

You and Mom certainly loved life and lived it to the fullest. You were such great partners! I loved Sunday mornings because that was the day we would go to church and Mom would prepare a big lunch. While it was being cooked, you guys would teach us kids to polka and waltz. That was so much fun! The two of you had so many friends and such an active social life that as adult kids we had to call ahead to schedule time on your calendar. I loved the way the two of you would interact; like when it came to discipline. If we were doing something we weren't supposed to do, Mom would always say, "Richard go discipline those kids." You would come in with a little grin and say, "let's settle down now" and leave. You were such a gentle spirit. I also liked how it seemed as though Mom would tell you what to do; she assured me though that in the end if it was something really important to you; you would do what you wanted to do. Just a bit stubborn I guess.

You also had a very unique quality in that while you had strong opinions on things, you were also very progressive (on most things!!) and willing to listen and accept new ideas. You were always very polite and treated people with respect. Even when you were so ill and in the hospital back in June, you would still say thank you to the doctors and nurses and were always grateful for their help. Through all the days of chemo and radiation you remained positive. I admired that about you. What is really cool is that on the rare occasion when you were having a tough time it did not last for long because you would quickly say, "that's enough feeling sorry for myself; no pity party here" and you would move on.

You are the best Dad a daughter could EVER have and in fact the best person I have ever met! I always knew that you loved me even though it wasn't until recent times that we were able to say the words and hug and kiss each other. I guess that was the Norwegian in us. I am thankful that we were able break through our stoic heritage!

I think I have figured out why God wanted to take you home and why you will fit in so well. You are a great carpenter, a good fisherman, and you love of kids. You and Mom will make wonderful angels. And so, I will reluctantly let you go and so as I say, "goodbye", I can hear Mom saying, "Hello, what took you so long!" I know I will see you one day in God's kingdom. Until then, I promise to keep your memories alive and ask you to watch over us from above.

My Father's Hands

My father's hands so strong and large; tell the story of a man, a father, and a friend. In their youth they played catch with siblings, passed footballs to teammates and fouled out playing basketball. They held Mom's hand in good times and bad; providing confidence and safety as only a Dad could. They fed, hugged, and played with us kids and were always teaching and showing us how to do "things".

My father's hands worked the land, milked the cows, tended to the pigs, roofed numerous buildings and waterproofed basements. They help start First Responders, answered pages, administered aid and performed CPR to all ages. They held golf clubs, shot two holes in one, planted the golf course flowers and challenged his partners. They fished the river and numerous lakes using every kind of bait and always provided the food for the fish fries while on vacation "Up North".

My father's hands steered Bus # 7 waving hello and good-bye for 53 years. They carved the wood and sanded the boards for Norwegian trunks, Tina boxes, furniture and "Pet Urns". They prayed and prayed, accepted communion and gave the sign of peace to friends and visitors. They shook thousands of hands, poured gallons of coffee, shuffled decks of cards, and beat grandchildren at Dominos.

Dad's dear friend and first responder colleague, Dorothy Jasperson, who worked at the local paper, the Westby Times also wrote several tributes to Dad reflecting her deep devotion and admiration.

Published – Wednesday, February 06, 2008

Richard Ekern wasn't just a bus driver in the Westby Area School District, he was a friend to all and like family to many. On Jan. 27, Ekern was honored by hundreds of people who waited in line for a chance to thank him for the positive influence he had on their children and in their own lives over the past five decades he spent driving bus.

At the age of 75, Ekern would be the first to tell you that he lived a good life and is thankful for all the blessings he's been granted. He married his high school sweetheart, Ilene and together they celebrated 55 years of wedded bliss before she passed away last August. Together the two of them raised four children, Reid (Nancy), Renee Joseph (Tom), Randy (Marna) and Todd (Vicki) and were blessed with grandchildren and great-grandchildren. He's loved, lost and learned to deal with life's unfortunate changes to the point where many people would have given up, but Ekern never did.

Ekern's life began changing in 2004 when he developed non-Hodgkin's lymphoma. He discovered a lump in his neck, which turned out to be one of many that had manifested themselves throughout his body. With an optimistic attitude toward life he placed his faith in God and the medical staff at Gundersen Lutheran's Cancer Center. Why not, he felt fine and he wasn't about to let a bout with cancer rock his world.

He started an intensive series of chemotherapy treatments to fight the cancer which had invaded his body. Unlike the majority of patients who have adverse side effects to the strong chemotherapy drugs, Ekern was one of the fortunate few who very seldom suffered from the nausea, vomiting and the days of total fatigue following a treatment. He lost his hair and was weak at times, but felt blessed to feel as good as he did.

As good as Ekern felt on the outside, the cancer on the inside refused to take a back seat to the medications which were being pumped through his veins or to be blinded by the radiation treatments which were designed to shrink the lingering tumors. Through it all he never gave up the fight. Ekern became one of only 41 people in the United States participating in a clinical trial designed to attack his form of cancer from a new direction. As promising as studies made it sound, the new treatment regimen backfired and left Ekern battling for his life and his survival in doubt.

After weeks of hospitalization in 2007, Ekern found a renewed inner strength and began to battle back. He spent month's recuperating under the watchful eye of beloved wife, family and friends. Then, without warning or even a good-bye, Ekern was forced to face the toughest battle of his life when his wife of 55 years died, leaving him without the love of his life to care for him and keep his spirit alive.

As hard as he tried to stay strong on the outside, inside his heart was broken and the cancer refused to take a back seat to his emotional pain. Ekern lost massive amounts of weight and continued to grow weaker as doctors struggled to find a cure. Throughout it all Ekern remained positive and devoted to driving school bus. After 53 years of driving he'd become a friend to hundreds of kids and a familiar face to families on Lovaas Ridge and down the winding roads of Spring Coulee along his route.

After losing his wife, driving school bus became his lifeline and gave Ekern a reason to keep up the fight. Then on Dec. 21, 2007, Ekern's lifeline was cut short when he turned over the keys to Bus #7, knowing in his heart that he was growing too weak to safely continue to drive.

For 53 years it was all part of the job he loved when he had to make a return trip to the Feller's residence to drop Herman off after he fell asleep in the seat on the bus yet again; when he was dropping off one of the first, second or third generation of the Bakkum family he'd hauled on his route over the years; when he was mending fences between students on the bus who just couldn't see eye to eye; when he making faces at kids just to see if they'd smile; when he was listening to the same joke he'd heard a hundred times before, but still reacting to the punch line like it was the first; when he was driving down a driveway beeping the horn so the kids knew he was there or if he was simply waving good-bye to parents as he drove away with a bus load of precious cargo; all that did matter is that he loved his job and all the families on his route will always hold *a special place in his heart.*

Ekern's devotion and love of his job were duly noted on Jan. 27 when he was recognized for his ability to teach students from the front of the bus, not from the front of the classroom. The students who rode Bus #7 surprised Ekern when he entered the doors of Westby Elementary School where they presented him with a photo album of memories and enough hugs and kisses to help mend part of his broken heart. Throughout the afternoon people reminisced and recanted colorful stories about the man they were there to honor.

Tears continued to well up in Ekern's eyes as he listened to the people speak so kindly about him. A humble man, with a heart of gold, he felt privileged to have had the opportunity to say good-bye, something many people never get the chance to do.

For Ekern attending the event held in his honor was his last unfinished business and he can go peacefully knowing that his kids miss him as much as he misses them, and that the parents who entrusted him with the most important people in their lives will be eternally grateful for the sense of security he provided them with for the past 53 years.

Ekern was also honored by the school district for his years of service to the community and when the party was over the entire room echoed a rowdy cheer of, 'Go Richard Go', as his family wheeled him home and he waved one last good-bye.

Below is her second tribute:

Saying good-bye isn't always easy, but still necessary

What's the point?

Most of us have lost a loved one at some point in our lives or know someone who has. For some the loss may have come as result of an unfortunate accident, while for others it came as a result of a disease which slowly destroys the human body and leaves on a shell when the end is near.

Regardless of the way a person dies, the end result always leaves the people left behind with unanswered questions and an empty feeling inside. Yet, the passing of that loved one should also be a gentle reminder of the importance of living life to the fullest while you can, and that heartache is part of dying the same way happiness is part of living.

For my dear friend, Richard Ekern who passed away on January 31st, the pain he felt in his heart after he lost his beloved wife of 55 years, Ilene, last August was far more unbearable than the cancer which consumed his body at the end.

She left him without saying good-bye, she left without kissing him good night; she left him with unanswered questions and she left him at a time in his life when he needed "his rock" to lean on. He never understood his loss, but he tried to accept it knowing in his heart that it was only a matter of time before he would hold her again.

He told me many times that he believes God has a plan and although we may not always agree with the process, that if we believe there is a light at the end of the tunnel that when we get to the other end, that love shines brighter than ever, life's pain disappears and that all those unanswered questions will be resolved.

This gentleman, with an infectious smile, touched many lives during his 75 years on earth. His love of children took him in the hearts of hundreds of families as a bus driver in the Westby Area School District for 53 years. His sense of community kept him an active member of the Westby First Responders since it was founded. His faith in God kept him involved in church and his love of life kept him strong, even when his disease made him feel weak.

It was Richard's strength that helped me get through my first emergency call as a first responder. The newest volunteer on the department at the time, and still wet behind the ears, he showed me that life's tragedies don't always have happy endings and that real life situations can't be taught in a classroom. He kept me focused and reassured me that everything would be okay as long as I didn't give up.

Richard was a role model to many, especially the kids on his bus. He's provided a friendly face when children needed it the most. He's read stories, poems and observed the artistic talents of kids who proudly handed him their creations for review when they hopped on board his school bus. He made sure kids were safely in their houses before departing for the next stop and always greeted them with a smile as they boarded and a wave when they left. He held the upper hand when he needed to make a point and he melted like a teddy bear when tears would flow.

In December, when his health deteriorated to the point he could no longer drive, Richards, sent a letter home to every family on his route thanking them for allowing him to spend time with their children. He told the kids how special they were to him, but most of all he reminded them to love themselves, get along and be happy no matter what road life takes them down.

Even tough cancer took its toll on his body, nothing could touch Richard's heart. He love life and all of its ups and downs; he loved visiting with people of all ages,; he loved woodcarving and found it relaxing; he loved golfing and was especially proud of his hole-in-one; he loved following high school sports and made a wonderful bleacher coach; he loved practical jokes and dressing up like a big kid at Halloween; he loved fishing on the river with friends; but most of all he loved spending time with family and friends.

His new journey has just begun. My wish for my friend is that when he gets to the end of the tunnel, may it be as bright as he made me believe, may all his questions have answers, may his heart be mended and may Ilene be the angel greeting him with open arms and once again kissing him good night.

You were a good man, who lived a full life. You will be sadly missed, but forever loved.

God Bless You Richard and Ilene, together again.

That's my point

Life if too short to wake up with regrets, so love the people who treat you right. Forget about the ones who don't. Believe everything happens for a reason. If you get a second chance, grab it with both hands. If it changes your life, let if. Nobody said life would be easy, they just promised it would be worth it. Author Unknown.

Almost two years later one of Dad's former students, Alexis Leum entered the Voice of Democracy Contest sponsored by Westby Veterans of Foreign Wars Post 8021 and Coon Creek VRW Post 10532. The theme of that year's competition was "does America Still Have Hero's? " Below is her submission:

> *Does America Still Have Hero's? Is so what defines a hero" What type of hero are people looking for? Many can find "super Heroes" like Batman, Cat Woman, and Flash Gordon in the movies but there is an everyday type of hero too. For an old lady, a little boy who helps her cross the street may be her hero or that same little boy's hero may be the firefighter who save him from a house fire. There are many different types of heroes in the world and they are all important.*
>
> *My hero was my bus driver. He passed away from cancer last year. Our bus had always been happy and we were all a family, we knew everyone who walked up the steps and who left. Every morning on the bus when he saw the kid's face, he said, "Good morning". He made every kid feel like someone cared and he did. He was always a thicker man so when he started chemo, he started growing really thin. No one really cared that he drove my dad and his siblings to school along with everyone else's parents. Everyone felt safe with him driving and felt that this man would live forever. During his chemo treatments, his wife died of a sudden death. Everyone missed him while he took some time off. Having a sub driver just wasn't the same. Toward the end of his battle with cancer, we made a poster that said" We love Bus #7 and had all the Bus #7 students hold the sign in front of the bus and gave him a photo. Well, the day we learned that he had passed, we were all horrified. That was the worst day so far in my whole life. But I will always remember my hero.*

It was so special and rewarding to see that my father's memory lives on. What a privilege to be his daughter!

Pictures by Dad's bus kids

Made in the USA
Columbia, SC
07 December 2018